Date Loaned

APR 2 M			
APR 16 ET			
MAY 26 ET			
AUG 24 1991			

THE
SCHUMPETERIAN
SYSTEM

THE SCHUMPETERIAN SYSTEM

By

RICHARD V. CLEMENCE

Assistant Professor of Economics
Wellesley College

and

FRANCIS S. DOODY

Associate Professor of Economics
Boston University
College of Business Administration

1950

ADDISON-WESLEY PRESS, INC.

CAMBRIDGE 42, MASS.

To Our Wives

PREFACE

The manuscript of this book was virtually completed at the time of Professor Schumpeter's death, and we have tried in the few remaining pages to proceed as if that shocking loss to our science had not already occurred. If we were to write the whole book over again, we should think it appropriate to express some of our ideas rather differently. This should be borne in mind by the reader, and he should interpret nothing he finds here as evidencing any want of respect to the memory of a great man.

It has become our responsibility to explain exactly what connection Professor Schumpeter himself had with this study, and the extent to which our findings may be said to have had his approval. Since both of us were students of his for some years, it will hardly be supposed that he exerted no influence on the contents of this book. He was, moreover, aware of the fact that we were writing it. From the time we began, however, we worked quite independently of his counsel, and he never saw any of our results. What we have to say, therefore, is said wholly on our own authority, and Professor Schumpeter's personal approval is claimed for none of it.

We have tried to make the argument in the text intelligible to undergraduate students; the footnotes are addressed primarily to more advanced scholars. Some references have been given in abbreviated form, since all the works cited are listed in full in the Bibliography.

Any married man with children who has ever written anything will take the dedication for granted.

R.V.C.
F.S.D.

CONTENTS

PART ONE: INTRODUCTION

PART TWO: EXPOSITION

PART THREE: CRITICISM

PART FOUR: CONCLUSION

Chapter 1

INTRODUCTION

The Schumpeterian System occupies a remarkable place in the history of economic thought. Almost from the beginning of his work on the theories of interest and of business cycles Professor Schumpeter saw a vision of a distinctly capitalist process taking place in historic time. His youthful vision, first reduced to a comprehensive model in 1911, has since been elaborated and refined, but it has been altered in no essential respect to the present day.[1] Such extraordinary consistency is almost unique in our science, and it is by no means a proof of virtue. What it rather suggests is that tests be made of the hypothesis that the model withstands critical attack. That is what we propose to do in this book.

For our present purpose there is no particular interest attaching to the sources of the ideas embodied in the Schumpeterian System. Like all system builders, Professor Schumpeter had many obligations to others, and anyone wishing to inform himself on the question will find that acknowledgments have been generously given. The question of "originality" is here, as elsewhere, irrelevant, for originality consists of the achievement of new combinations, and not of the creation of something out of nothing.

The focus of our attention will be a comparatively small body of literature. There is, first, the *Theorie der wirtschaftlichen Entwicklung,* published originally in the fall of 1911,[2] and translated

---

[1] There is some discussion of Professor Schumpeter's earlier work in H. S. Ellis, *German Monetary Theory, 1905-1933,* especially Chapter XVIII. Compare also A. H. Hansen, *Business Cycle Theory,* and T. Suranyi-Unger, *Economics in the Twentieth Century.*

[2] The first German edition carries the date 1912. Professor Schumpeter is, however, the authority for the date here given. See *The Theory of Economic Development,* p. ix.

from the edition of 1926 with negligible changes as *The Theory of Economic Development* (1934).[3] Next, there are a few articles[4] published after 1926; these will, however, be hardly more than mentioned. We shall above all be concerned with *Business Cycles* (1939), subtitled *A Theoretical, Historical, and Statistical Analysis of the Capitalist Process,* in which the Schumpeterian System is displayed in its final form. *Capitalism, Socialism, and Democracy* (1942, 1947) completes our list.

In comparison with the systems of such scholars as Toynbee and Spengler, the Schumpeterian System has very modest dimensions. No effort is made to achieve a synthesis of world history or even of the history of Western civilization. On the contrary, the whole analysis is concerned with the economic aspects of capitalist society, and most of the resources of modern economics are brought to bear on the comparatively narrow problem of the economic process of the capitalist era. Not only economics, but other social sciences as well are drawn upon heavily in the attempt to develop a model of this process. The important question, however, is not what resources are utilized but what results are achieved, and the present study is part of an effort to find out.

In recent years the Schumpeterian System has been the object of an interest amounting nearly to apathy. We may well begin by considering why this has been so. The most obvious answer is that the major treatise appeared at the wrong time, and that everyone was too busy explaining what Keynes had tried to say to have energies for much else. There is surely truth in this, and the fact that *Business Cycles* contained no running commentary on the *General Theory* meant that it was not required reading for many people. Moreover, to read Professor Schumpeter's two volumes with any care

---

[3] The German edition is not widely accessible, and a careful comparison with the translation has shown that nothing would be gained by citing the original in this book. Mr. Opie's rendition is admirable, and the English edition moreover contains a new Preface and some additional contributions by the author. Our references will hence be made to that version.

[4] For us, the most important of these are "The Explanation of the Business Cycle," *Economica,* December, 1927; "The Instability of Capitalism," *Economic Journal,* September, 1928; and "The Analysis of Economic Change," *Review of Economic Statistics,* May, 1935. Others that shed light on various aspects of the Schumpeterian System are listed in the Bibliography of this book.

would take much more time and effort than were needed to get through the *General Theory*.[5] What to many was still worse, the reader of *Business Cycles* would discover no positive program there, and not much in the way of hints on what to do to be saved. Indeed, the familiar music of an axe being sharpened on a grindstone was altogether missing from Professor Schumpeter's composition.

In the face of such difficulties, the burden on reviewers was extraordinarily great, and it is not surprising that they failed to rise to the occasion. Reviews of *Business Cycles* rivalled those of the *General Theory* in confusion,[6] with the difference that there were no outstanding exceptions to the rule.[7] The impression thus prevailed from the outset that in view of everything the book was hardly worth bothering about just then, and little attention has been paid to it since.[8] In textbooks, the Schumpeterian System

---

[5] Compare E. G. Bennion, "Unemployment in the Theories of Schumpeter and Keynes," *American Economic Review*, June, 1943, p. 337n.

[6] The most considerable review, both in length and in influence, was the article by Professor Kuznets, "Schumpeter's Business Cycles," *American Economic Review*, June, 1940, pp. 257-271. This is the only review of *Business Cycles* included in the long bibliography compiled by Professor Somers for *Readings in Business Cycle Theory*, whereas virtually all the reviews of the *General Theory* are listed.

Some of the reviews of *Business Cycles* raised points that will be discussed in the text. Those not mentioned elsewhere include a number that appeared in the leading journals. J. Marshak (*Journal of Political Economy*, December, 1940, pp. 889-894) made an attempt to express the model in terms of a few simple equations, admittedly without much success. O. Morgenstern (*Journal of the American Statistical Association*, June, 1940, pp. 423-424) had space for only a brief and noncritical note, as did M. G. K. (Kendall?) in the *Journal of the Royal Statistical Society*, Vol. CIV, Part II, 1941, pp. 177-180. H. A. Innis (*Canadian Journal of Economics and Political Science*, February, 1940, pp. 90-96) stressed the historical aspects of the analysis. The point about gold discoveries raised by Professor Innis on page 95 of his review is of some importance from standpoints other than ours, but does not extend to the validity of the essential interpretation.

[7] Recall, for example, what Professor Lerner did for Keynes in the pages of the *International Labour Review*.

[8] The Schumpeterian influence is, however, apparent in the work of the Research Center in Entrepreneurial History at Harvard. See *Change and the Entrepreneur*, Preface, p. v, for their acknowledgment.

Any statement that literature has been neglected must naturally be supposed to except Professor Marget, whose *Theory of Prices* covers everything relevant to his subject. His second volume, in particular, shows that none

receives scant mention, and it is usually identified as one more theory of cycles[9] on a par with many others. In histories of economic thought the model is presented either in severely attenuated form or not at all. Essays are written and accepted as original contributions though they deal with subjects treated exhaustively in *Business Cycles*, and considerable studies of Professor Schumpeter's very problem are produced without much evidence that their authors are aware that his treatise exists.[10]

During the past decade and a half there has been a tendency for national income analysis to overshadow, if not to supplant the study of business cycles.[11] An extreme manifestation of this tendency is the comforting belief that business cycles are now a thing of the

---

of the monetary aspects of the Schumpeterian System, if indeed any others, has escaped his attention. Unfortunately, however, Professor Marget's treatise is itself a neglected work.

[9] An effort to avoid this outcome came to nothing. Compare N. Mirkowich, "Schumpeter's Theory of Economic Development," *American Economic Review*, September, 1940, p. 580.

[10] The statements made in the text are doubtless common knowledge, and we shall confine ourselves to a few outstanding examples. These are merely illustrative; the list could be prolonged almost indefinitely.

The standard theoretical work, *Prosperity and Depression*, contains only brief references to the Schumpeterian System.

Among textbooks, J. F. Due, *Intermediate Economic Analysis*, pp. 400-401, classifies the theory of innovation with weather and psychological theories of cycles as insufficiently important to deserve more than mention.

Checking the index references to Schumpeter in such popular histories of thought as those of Haney, Gide and Rist, Roll, and Whittaker, is not a profitable employment.

Examples of essays of the sort referred to will be found in Part III of this book.

In *Value and Capital*, great stress is laid on the importance of innovation in the trade cycle, but no reference is made to Professor Schumpeter's work.

Of eighteen indexed references to Schumpeter in *A Survey of Contemporary Economics*, fourteen are to publications other than *Business Cycles*, and the other four are unrewarding.

Neither C. E. Ayres, *Theory of Economic Progress*, nor H. G. Moulton, *Controlling Factors in Economic Development*, contains a single mention of Professor Schumpeter's treatise.

[11] When we proposed some eight years ago that the national income be made the center of attention in the teaching of economics, such a shift of emphasis was the reverse of our intent. That the Schumpeterian System was not widely known was brought home to us by the immediate assumption of our readers that we were disciples of Keynes.

past, and that government, with one hand on the economic steering wheel, can keep the car of progress out of the ditch.   An overwhelming triumph of conventional income analysis and the corollary principle of effective demand would, however, be a costly victory.[12] The economics of the steering wheel is akin to prescription without diagnosis, and the smothering of symptoms does not necessarily constitute adequate treatment.   The aggregative approach has serious limitations, and the ease with which euthanasia is mistaken for remedy is not the least of them.   Moreover, it should be remembered that the principle of effective demand is essentially a static concept, and that it sheds but little light on the dynamics of reality. Without business cycle analysis, our efforts at control cannot be very effective nor can their implications be clearly understood.   The particular elements within our aggregates are as important as ever, and little is to be gained by pretending otherwise.

Indications are not lacking that there is a growing awareness of the inadequacies of macrostatics,[13] and there are even some signs that a Counter Revolution is in prospect.   With the disillusionment of a generation trained in the new orthodoxy, the Schumpeterian System acquires increasing significance.   Since the publication of the major treatise, however, a set of "standard criticisms" [14] has grown up that not only discourages investigation of the model but threatens to become a part of the folklore of economics.

In economics, as in other fields, ideas have a tendency to live lives of their own, and having become a part of tradition, they are very difficult to root out.   When summarized in a few neat words or phrases, these gems of wisdom become substitutes for thought, and gradually take on much of the status of revealed truth.   Occasionally, some iconoclast sees fit to challenge one of them, and a brief

---

[12] Compare J. Marshak, "A Cross Section of Business Cycle Discussion," *American Economic Review,* June, 1945, pp. 377-379.
[13] The method is, however, coming to be looked upon with favor by some economic historians.   Compare T. S. Ashton, "The Relation of Economic History to Economic Theory," *Economica,* May, 1946, p. 92.   Professor Ashton attaches considerable importance to the role of the interest rate in his *Industrial Revolution.*   While this is a minor defect in a book that approaches perfection, any strenuous effort to rewrite economic history in terms of the *General Theory* seems likely to have serious consequences.
[14] The term is Professor Lange's.   See O. Lange, Review of *Business Cycles, Review of Economic Statistics,* November, 1941, p. 192.

flurry ensues, after which things go on about as before.   It is easy to think of plenty of ideas that are passing, if they have not already passed, beyond the stage of effective discussion.   Consider, for instance, the status of questions like these:

Did Marshall's *Principles* represent a synthesis of the Classicals with Jevons and the Austrians?   What is the Keynes-Hansen School? Did the Classical economists assume continuous full employment? What pre-Keynesian economists believed in Say's Law?   Is innovation an important element in Keynes's trade cycle theory?   But there is no need to continue.   It is apparent that the standard criticisms of the Schumpeterian System must be examined soon, if they are to be examined effectively at all, and if discussion is to yield any substantial results.

The Schumpeterian System is an imposing analytical machine.   It is large enough; it has sufficient power; and it is made of the best materials.   But will it work?   So its inventor claims, but others are less confident.   Indeed, it is said that there are serious flaws in all parts of the engine, and that it can never be made to operate.   Let us examine the System for ourselves, and see what conclusions we can reach.

PART TWO: EXPOSITION

INTRODUCTION

The three chapters immediately following present a highly con-
densed summary of the Schumpeterian System. This summary is
meant to be more than an outline or sketch of the model; our intention has been to compress the entire schema into a few pages. No
one knows better than we do that such an objective cannot be fully
realized. We have come as close to it as we can, but we have had
to leave out numerous refinements, qualifications, and sidelights
that represent altogether a considerable loss. Important details
omitted from this exposition will, however, be developed in the
remainder of the book.

We have done our best throughout these expository chapters to
render Professor Schumpeter's meaning, and nothing in them should
be interpreted as comment of our own. All statements are either
taken verbatim from *Business Cycles,* or reduce long passages in that
book to a few words. We were obliged to abandon an attempt to
cite references in this part of our study, since it quickly became clear
that several would have to be given for many individual words and
phrases. The use of special punctuation to enclose direct quotations was impracticable for a similar reason.

The following exposition of the Schumpeterian System furnishes
the background for the subsequent discussion. We hope that from
these few pages the reader will be able to get a clear picture of the
model as a whole, and of the relations of the separate parts of it to
the whole and to one another. The memories of those already
familiar with the schema may thus be refreshed, and others may
survey the entire terrain before plunging into dark thickets and
fording difficult streams.

Chapter 2 deals with the Pure Model of the Schumpeterian System
in which a two-phase business cycle is obtained by the introduction
of an innovation into a situation of general equilibrium. Chapter 3

presents the Second Approximation in which the Secondary Wave is developed, and in which additional facts are introduced, yielding a four-phase cycle approximating reality. With Chapter 4 the Multicycle Schema is reached, and cycles of various types emerge from the innovating process.

Chapter 2

THE PURE MODEL

The Pure Model has as its basis an economic system in general equilibrium. All economic activity in the model is essentially repetitive, following the course of familiar routine, and the model may thus be regarded as a circular flow of economic life. Every firm in the system is in perfect competitive equilibrium, with its costs, consisting of wages and rents, exactly equal to its receipts. Prices everywhere are equated to average costs; profits are zero; profit opportunities are nonexistent; interest rates are zero; and there is no involuntary unemployment of resources. Every household, like every firm, is in full long-run equilibrium, with receipts equal to expenditures, and with a budgetary pattern that cannot, under the existing circumstances, be advantageously altered.

Into this system of synchronized adjustment an innovation intrudes. This innovation consists of a new production function introduced by an entrepreneur with a view to making money profits. It is assumed that such an innovation always entails the construction of new plant and equipment, requiring non-negligible time and outlay. Moreover, it is supposed that a new firm is always founded for the purpose, and that this invariably involves the rise of a new man or men to business leadership.

These entrepreneurs belong to a distinct class in the sense that they possess, in more than ordinary degree, the ability to visualize profit possibilities in unproved commodities, organizations, methods, markets, and so on, and to overcome the obstacles that may stand in the way of getting new things done. This talent is by no means rare, but is in some degree common to most of the population. The majority of would-be entrepreneurs, however, never get their projects in motion, and many of those who do manage to found a firm fail to realize any profits. In the Pure Model such errors are assumed to be absent.

Innovation is financed in the Pure Model by the creation of bank credit. The special function of bankers in the system is viewed as the appraisal of the prospects of new ventures, and the provision of new funds for such entrepreneurs as merit encouragement. Since the financing of innovation requires that entrepreneurs and bankers agree that profit prospects are favorable under existing circumstances, interest emerges in the form of a charge made for the extension of credit. Interest is thus a monetary phenomenon linked to innovation, and the interest rate is tied to the rate of profit.

With newly created purchasing power at his disposal, the entrepreneur is able to bid productive services away from their current uses. Thus the output of producers' goods increases, while that of consumers' goods decreases. In real terms the new firm is established at the expense of those already in existence, although profits of the old firms will increase because the additional consumer spending is devoted to a smaller output.

The first entrepreneur to enter a new field must overcome all the obstacles that lie in the way of an untried project. The first new firm, however, smooths the path for others, and entrepreneurial activity takes place in a wave that exhausts the opportunities for gain. As borrowing diminishes, and as the earlier firms begin to repay bank loans, monetary expansion gives way to autodeflation at the same time that the output of the new enterprises is beginning to compete strongly with that of the old. The whole economy has now to undergo a process of readjustment before a new circular flow of routine activity can be established. As the adaptation to the changed situation occurs, some firms and industries expand into the new economic space created by development, others modernize, rationalize, or reconstruct, while still others that have now become obsolete pass from the scene altogether. The revision of values characteristic of disequilibrium increases the difficulty of planning and the risk of failure, leading to a further slackening of entrepreneurial activity.

Innovation in the Pure Model yields a two-phase cycle of prosperity and recession, succeeded by the appearance of a new equilibrium from which the process may again be set in motion. Comparing the second equilibrium with the first, we find that the total output of the system is both greater and different in composition. The aggregate of money incomes is the same as before, but the price level is lower, and the price structure is altered to a new pattern. Households, which play only a passive role in the process, typically lose ground in prosperity as consumers' goods output diminishes and prices rise. In recession, however, the households are rewarded, as output increases beyond the original equilibrium level and prices decline. The terms prosperity and recession do not carry the same connotations for welfare that public opinion assigns to them. The seed is sown in prosperity and the harvest reaped in recession.

The Pure Model illustrates the capitalist process as it would work out in the absence of errors and speculative activities. The two-phase cycle has no particular periodicity, and the length of time occupied by the wave of prosperity and recession depends on the nature of the innovation introduced, and the structure of the system that is required to adapt itself.

The model and its working are strongly institutional in character. Definite types of private property and private initiative are assumed; a money and banking system with definite standards and traditions is taken for granted; and a definite scheme of motivation is above all presupposed. The analysis may properly be called historical in the sense that it is relevant to the conditions of a specific epoch, and its object is primarily to shed light on the economic process of the capitalist era.

Chapter 3

THE SECOND APPROXIMATION

Since the Pure Model is designed to demonstrate only the fundamental relationships between capitalist development and cyclical fluctuations, a number of important features remain to be added before the system can be regarded as a tolerable approximation to reality. The Second Approximation is the result of inserting the following elements into the primary pattern:

A. The Secondary Wave
B. Five additional facts completing the approximation
    1. Successive fluctuations
    2. Growth
    3. The spreading of credit creation
    4. Induced investment
    5. Imperfections of competition and of equilibrium

The Secondary Wave

The Secondary Wave, which tends to stand out quantitatively above the primary one that carries it, includes the phenomena of direct reactions to the primary wave and of speculative activities induced by it, together with the consequences of these phenomena.

As innovations are embodied in new plant and equipment, the additional spending of firms is followed almost immediately by additional consumer outlay. The increasing demand for the output of old firms leads to attempts at expanding production. In addition to this direct reaction, many people will undertake ventures that promise to be successful only on the assumption that the current rate of expansion will continue. Price speculation thus appears on the scene, and innovations that could not have yielded profits under equilibrium conditions are now introduced. The errors and excesses that were absent from the Pure Model are inherent in the processes of the Secondary Wave, which thus contains those aspects of generality that tend to obscure the fundamental

12

phenomena igniting and supporting the larger activity. Prosperity readily develops into boom proportions, and the most prominent features of the general expansion may be far removed from the underlying process.

The Secondary Wave, however conspicuous it may be, has little or no driving force of its own, and a turn in the primary wave will induce a break in the secondary prosperity. When this break comes, the material for a cumulative contraction is present, and recession is not only a phase of readjustment, but involves as well the liquidation of numerous untenable positions. Recession no longer leads directly to a new equilibrium, as in the Pure Model, but may instead give way to depression as the system outruns its equilibrium neighborhood. Not only are speculative ventures of the boom now liquidated, but it is also probable that many sound positions will deteriorate and even collapse. As the abnormal liquidation runs its course, readjustments are gradually made, and the struggle toward a new equilibrium produces recovery or revival.

With the introduction of the Secondary Wave, we arrive at a four-phase cycle consisting of two essential phases of prosperity and recession, a pathological phase of depression and, following depression, a necessary phase of revival. Depressions are pathological in the sense that they play no indispensable role in the capitalist process, which would be logically complete without them. No theoretical expectations can be formed for the occurrence and severity of depressions, for the course of events will depend on the extent of the maladjustments that exist, and on the particular reactions that happen to take place. It is not even certain that, historically, depression will always follow prosperity and recession, and only a detailed investigation of an actual period can show whether or not depression was present.

When depression does occur, it gradually wears off as liquidation is accomplished with diminishing repercussions and diffused effects, and as depression business emerges to create new opportunities for certain firms. The lower turning point may be described conveniently in terms of self-generating accounts of the cycle, which stress the details of the readjustments brought on by the collapse of the Secondary Wave. In the most general case, however, there is no certainty about recovery. None of these phenomena are, moreover, relied upon to carry the system beyond recovery and into prosperity, for prosperity develops once more only if innovating activity is renewed.

The equilibrium neighborhood that constitutes the destination of the economy after depression differs in two respects from that which would have been reached without abnormal liquidation. First, the ability of a given firm to survive abnormal liquidation depends mainly on its financial support. Sound ventures that would have succeeded in the Pure Model may be brought down by the break of the Secondary Wave, at the same time that enterprises without such claims to survival manage to stay on their feet. Second, an appreciable interval is required for the two lower phases to run their course. The data of the system necessarily change during this time, introducing different elements to which the economy must adjust.

The four-phase cycle of prosperity, recession, depression, and revival bears a strong superficial resemblance to that identified by many students of time series. One important difference from some theories should be noted at this point. In the Schumpeterian System every cycle is a historical individual, and not a unit to be marked off at the convenience of the observer. It is therefore theoretically wrong to count off cycles in a series from peak to peak or from trough to trough; a complete unit covers the interval between the equilibrium neighborhood preceding prosperity and the succeeding equilibrium neighborhood following revival. Unless cycles are correctly counted, the fundamental difference between the propelling factors in revival and prosperity is necessarily lost.

A few other facts must now be added to the Secondary Wave in order to complete the Second Approximation.

SUCCESSIVE FLUCTUATIONS

For convenience of exposition it was originally assumed that the cycle under discussion was the first of its kind, and that it was thus unaffected by the results of previous development. It is now recognized that every prosperity, although it starts from an equilibrium neighborhood, originates in an atmosphere of imperfect routine containing innovations incompletely worked out, undigested elements of previous cycles, faulty adjustments resulting from errors, and so on.

With successive fluctuations incorporated into the system, it may be assumed that producers learn from experience to provide for the peak demands of prosperity, and that productive capacity, especially in the equipment industries, will be built with a view to full utilization only at such times. It follows that, in contrast to the Pure Model, output will expand more readily in prosperity, with costs and prices rising more slowly than they otherwise would. Moreover, the conditions for a special sort of short-run unemployment are thus created.

GROWTH

Growth is defined as changes in population, and in total savings and accumulations of households and firms respectively, corrected for variations in the purchasing power of the monetary unit. Growth has so far been excluded from the system on the ground that changes in population and in saving can be currently absorbed without giving rise to cyclical fluctuations. Cycles can be understood without Growth, but not *vice versa,* and the quantitative importance of Growth, especially of saving, is due to the process of capitalist development. Such saving, of course, may be used to finance innovation, although not without effects on economic contours, such as those of price levels.

THE SPREADING OF CREDIT CREATION

Credit creation in the Pure Model has its logical source in the financing of innovation. In the Secondary Wave, credit creation tends to lose its relation to innovation and becomes an instrument for financing business in general. Hence, the volume of credit creation in the Second Approximation will display variations not accounted for by the theory of the primary wave.

When ordinary business recovers in revival, credit creation is likely to expand as increasing output is financed. In recession it is quite possible that autodeflation will be negligible, since some entrepreneurs may not repay all they borrow and since banks as a whole may shift from the financing of innovation to the provision of purchasing power for old firms that are adapting themselves to the effects of recent innovation or expanding into new economic space created by it.

INDUCED INVESTMENT

The investment opportunities created by innovation are limited neither to the innovating industries themselves nor to the larger circle of such industries and their satellites.   Nor is induced investment confined to the exploitation of opportunities opened by the expansion of aggregate monetary demand.   An innovation in the field of transportation, for example, may create important investment opportunities in the building industry.   Moreover, increased output in one sphere may open new economic space in quite another by calling forth additional production to pay for it.   This is particularly likely to be characteristic of much activity in recession and revival.

IMPERFECTIONS OF COMPETITION AND OF EQUILIBRIUM

The most powerful influence responsible for the imperfections of competition in the real world is the capitalist process itself.   Other imperfections of both competition and equilibrium, however, exist, and the recognition of this, in addition to the imperfections resulting from previous fluctuations, completes the framework of the Second Approximation.   Thus, the assumptions of perfect competition and perfect equilibrium made at the outset must be dropped altogether.

The general effect of inserting these imperfections into the system as independent variables is to render analysis less neat and precise than it would otherwise have been.   One definite theoretical expectation is at the same time introduced.   Industries, even in equilibrium, may now be producing under conditions of decreasing average cost, and in all phases of the cycle except prosperity expectation is for this rather than for the opposite possibility.

Imperfections of competition and of equilibrium, as well as external factors, may account for unemployed resources independently of the cyclical process of development.   Since imperfections arise also from the evolutionary process, it must be recognized that full employment of resources now ceases to be a property of states of equi-

librium, but rather reflects disequilibrium of a certain type.   Equilibrium, again, is not to be found at cyclical peaks.   Apart from
rigidities, however, unemployment of resources is held to be incompatible with perfect competition and perfect equilibrium.

Chapter 4

THE MULTICYCLE SCHEMA

Multiple cycles, rather than a single wave, are suggested by this theory. There are three principal reasons to expect that the cycles generated by innovation would be of different types. These may be summarized as follows:

1. Different innovations would naturally require different lengths of time for their introduction. Some would necessitate the construction of a considerable amount of new plant and equipment, whereas others would require comparatively little. Furthermore, those innovations representing major improvements in the productive process would be expected to require a substantial period of time both to achieve general acceptance and to exert their influence on the economy as a whole. Innovations of a less fundamental character should, on the other hand, be accomplished more quickly, and they should produce more moderate and more rapid adjustments in those parts of the system that they primarily affect.

These considerations imply the existence of fluctuations of different average periodicity, and affect the nature of the relationship between them. As the waves of longer span develop their prosperity phases, the shorter fluctuations should rise more easily than they otherwise could, and depression phases of the minor cycles should be at least partially absorbed by the underlying expansion. When, on the contrary, the longer waves are passing through a depression phase, the prosperities of the shorter cycles might be largely concealed from view, and the changing phases of these minor fluctuations might be detected only by the moderation or intensification of the major depression. To understand or even to identify one type of cycle, it would therefore be necessary to take account of the phases of other cycles in which the given fluctuation was running its course.

2. Some innovations might produce a sequence of cycles all of the same type. There is no reason to suppose that the successive cycles of a series are always quite independent of one another.

Rather, it is more likely that after a given innovation has been successfully accomplished, the next will develop in the same or a closely related field.

History provides a number of obvious examples of this sort of phenomenon. Railroad construction proceeded in a series of steps, with only one or a few lines built at a time, and with reaction and absorption of effects separating the periods of expanding activity. Similarly, the automobile acquired its present importance by a sequence of advances in which a changing environment, including a new highway network as only one element, was both a result and a condition of achievement. The family resemblance of these series of cycles tends to weld them into a higher unit that will stand out as a historical individual.

3. A number of innovations may be interdependent, forming part of a larger process that represents a real phenomenon in itself. History again supplies examples. The Industrial Revolution, for instance, was composed of a number of cycles of different span superimposed on one another. At the same time, the whole economic and social framework of society was undergoing a significant transformation, a change that itself had some cyclical characteristics.

This sort of wave is different from both the types previously discussed. On the one hand, it cannot be identified with a specific class of innovation as distinct from others introduced during the same period. On the other hand, it is a real phenomenon and not the mere effect of a series of innovations more closely associated with one another than with others outside the sequence.

For these three reasons, then, the theory implies the existence of an indeterminate number of simultaneous cycles rather than a simple series of successive fluctuations. All cycles are, however, so far supposed to be of a general character. That is to say, the theory does not lead to the expectation that a separate cycle exists for each industry, or for each sector of the economy, but only that the fluctuations affecting the whole system are substantially different in origin and in length. Special cycles, such as those to be found in agriculture, are not excluded, but these are separate phenomena that do not necessarily fall within the field of expectation from the general theory.

Although a multiple-cycle hypothesis might have been made a part of the Schumpeterian System itself, this has not in fact been done. The question is instead left open beyond the point at which a refusal to accept the single-cycle hypothesis becomes necessary. In other words, the presence or absence of multiple cycles remains to be established by statistical and historical investigation.

The number of cycles to be identified becomes, then, in part, a question of descriptive convenience. Since tolerable data barely exist for a span of a century and a half, it is clear that any major movements to be discovered must be relatively few. At the same time, it is equally apparent that the search for minor types of fluctuations would be unlikely to be profitable after the most obvious had been recognized. Tentative identification of five cycle-types, and attempts to work out a statistical and historical analysis in terms of these, led to the conclusion that accuracy was insufficiently improved to warrant such a manifold classification. Three types of fluctuations were finally settled upon as being the minimum number that would permit an adequate exposition, and the maximum that could be conveniently handled. The three-cycle schema remains, however, a strictly practical device, and the theory is quite independent of it.

The long, medium, and short cycles chosen are those that have already acquired statistical and historical meaning, and that are particularly associated with the names of Kondratieff, Juglar, and Kitchin respectively. Respective average periodicities are roughly fifty-five years, between nine and ten years, and somewhat less than forty months; no strict regularity is implied.

Although the choice of three orders of cycles to represent an indefinite number of cycle types is a decision that owes nothing to the theory itself, the relationships among multiple cycles nevertheless form an integral part of the Schumpeterian System. As the reasons for expecting multiplicity of cycles indicate, the three types of fluctuation are not to be regarded as independent movements, but must on the contrary bear definite relationships to one another. Details apart, these relationships may be stated in terms of equilibrium tendencies.

Outside the circular flow of the Pure Model, the economy can, of course, never achieve general equilibrium. The concept, however, finds its practical application in the recognition of equilibrium neighborhoods in which the system is closer to general equilibrium than it is elsewhere. The closest approach to such equilibrium is at the close of the recovery phase of the Kondratieff. At other times, the disequilibrium of the economy as a whole from the standpoint of the Kondratieffs is a conditioning element for the Juglar fluctuations, and affects the larger business atmosphere in which they run their course. What passes for equilibrium in the Juglars is thus a partial adjustment in which the system absorbs only the more immediate effects of recent innovation, setting the stage for further innovation and Juglar prosperity. Whether Juglar prosperities are more or less intense than Juglar depressions depends on the phase of the Kondratieff in which they occur. In other words, the characteristics of the Juglars reflect the extent of the more fundamental maladjustments that have accumulated in the economy, and that must eventually be liquidated. In statistical time series the Kondratieff waves may be thought of as representative of a trend about which the Juglars fluctuate.

The relation of the Kitchin cycles to the Juglars is similar to that between the Juglars and the Kondratieffs. Because of the relatively large number of Kitchins, and the shortness of their average duration, the possibility must be left open that a definite historical association of particular innovation with a specific Kitchin may be not only unprovable, but nonexistent. Indeed, the Kitchins may well be fluctuations of the adaptive type.

The interrelationships among the simultaneous fluctuations require that each longer cycle should contain an integral number of shorter cycles. This necessity is not occasioned by the three-cycle schema; it is imposed by the theory itself. It does not follow, however, that this integral number should be always the same. Historically, nevertheless, it appears that there have been six Juglars in each Kondratieff, and three Kitchins in each Juglar. Expectation from the theory would be for less regularity.

PART THREE: CRITICISM

INTRODUCTION

In the following chapters we attempt to examine all the major objections to the Schumpeterian System that have been published in the English and American literature, and to deal briefly with some minor ones as well. A few of the points mentioned may even strike the reader as trivial, but they are included on the ground that a number of trivialities taken together add up to something important. It is, moreover, hard to be sure that any objection deserves to be ignored altogether, particularly when it is linked with the name of some prominent economist.

We have tried to render the views of each critic accurately and in as much detail as space would permit. Direct quotations have been presented wherever possible, but these may not be wholly reliable when removed from their original context. Where criticisms have been insufficiently concise to admit of reproduction verbatim some degree of misrepresentation is still more likely. For such errors as have occurred we tender our apologies in advance.

This study is concerned with ideas rather than with men. The authors of all criticisms have been identified in order to assure the reader that we are not manufacturing objections of our own on which to exercise our ingenuity. It is, however, the ideas themselves in which we are interested insofar as they may be said to have an independent existence.

We have grouped the criticisms of the Schumpeterian System under the following six headings: The Circular Flow, The Concept of Innovation, The Clustering of Innovations, The Impact of Innovation, The Three-Cycle Schema, and The Long Waves. These headings supply the chapter titles of Part III.

Chapter 5

THE CIRCULAR FLOW

The analytical foundation of the Schumpeterian System is the concept of a circular flow of economic activity reproducing itself continuously at a constant rate through time. The principal objections to this conception fall into three categories, which may be summarized as follows:

1. First, there is the purely theoretical problem of a zero rate of interest. Since everyone agrees that the existence of a zero rate in the world of reality is, to say the least, highly unlikely, the issue reduces to the question of whether or not such a rate is the logical consequence of the conditions under which the circular flow is assumed to operate. It is, of course, not quite true to say that a zero, or even a negative rate of interest is altogether unknown in the real world, but we shall take it for granted that the irrelevance of such special cases to the present discussion is self-evident.

2. Second, the circular flow is a model of a purely competitive system. In order to establish his stationary process, Professor Schumpeter has assumed away the monopolistic restrictions and market imperfections that form a large part of both the actual world and theories that are designed to explain it. Despite all the theoretical contributions in connection with which the names of Professor Chamberlin and Mrs. Robinson are only two of the most prominent, the Schumpeterian circular flow in its most recent formulation remains essentially what it was in 1911.

3. Third, the data of the circular flow include a structure of economic society that is supposed to be characteristic of capitalism. Even assuming that the model is itself analytically valid, we may still question the validity of the structure on which it is based. If capitalist society is not tolerably approximated by the institutional arrangements underlying the circular flow, then the Schumpeterian System is defective from the beginning. Moreover, the changes that would be required to bring the model into closer conformity with

reality might produce a quite different type of circular flow, with perhaps radically altered implications for the theory of economic development.

With the nature and relevance of these issues thus briefly indicated, we may proceed to deal with them systematically. First, however, it may be well to clear the ground for the discussion by examining in more detail the place of the circular flow in the Schumpeterian System, and the assumptions upon which it rests. This roundabout approach ought, on Böhm-Bawerkian principles, to be more productive than a direct attack on the problem.

We may begin by observing that the notion of something like a circular flow of economic activity must always have been held by economists from the earliest days of our science. We have only to remind ourselves of the Physiocratic efforts at model-building; the classical stationary states of Smith, Ricardo, and Mill; and the long-run equilibrium of Alfred Marshall [1] in order to recognize that the concept has sufficiently distinguished predecessors. One need not be a professional theorist in order to appreciate the necessity for envisioning at least a rudimentary system of interdependent incomes, costs, and prices in order to think about an economy at all. It is true that agreement terminates at an early stage, and that theoretical refinements do not seem equally important to everyone. Those who take their theory seriously, however, regard the work of Leon Walras as a notable achievement, though it was hardly more than a start toward satisfactory equilibrium analysis.

The Schumpeterian version of Walrasian equilibrium is a model of a closed domain in which every economic subject has so perfectly adapted his behavior to his environment that there is no further incentive to change. This means, not that no decisions have to be made and no activities undertaken, but only that the decisions made in each period of account reproduce those of preceding periods and imply the same behavior.

[1] If Marshall's long-run equilibrium is assumed to hold for every unit in the system, we have the equivalent of Walrasian equilibrium. The minimum rate of profit included in the cost curves of partial equilibrium analysis naturally becomes zero as soon as we extend the analysis to the whole system. That Marshall was no stranger to the concept of general equilibrium is clear from his review of Jevons, as Keynes pointed out. See J. M. Keynes, "Alfred Marshall, 1842-1924," *Memorials of Alfred Marshall*, p. 42. The passage from Marshall's review may be found on p. 94 of the same book.

The result may be reached analytically[2] by starting from a given group of economic subjects inhabiting a given area.   These people, having at their disposal limited resources, proceed on the basis of whatever preferences they may happen to have, and such knowledge of productive techniques as they possess, to make the best of their situation.   Assuming the existence of such capitalist institutions as private property, competitive private enterprise, and free markets, we find the solution to be a stationary state in which every firm produces its output at a constant rate in a plant of optimum size employing the best known methods of combining resources.   All prices are equated to minimum unit costs, and the receipts of each firm resolve themselves into wages and rents, leaving no profits other than wages of management.   Since no firm could expand without incurring losses, there is no motivation for business borrowing, and hence no interest rate exists other than zero.   Money is, in the immortal words of Mill, "a machine for doing quickly and commodiously, what would be done, though less quickly and commodiously, without it." [3]   Since every household, like every firm, is in stationary equilibrium, even household borrowing and lending may be ruled out.   Alternatively, of course, it may be allowed for under such special circumstances as we may suppose to give rise to it.   The point is simply that nothing essential is changed by eliminating such possibilities altogether.

Since any good textbook will supply the technical details omitted from this brief sketch,[4] we may leave these matters to one side and pass on to something of more immediate importance.   The Walrasian approach, we should observe, is not the only route by which the circular flow may be reached.   We may instead start from an existing exchange economy, and inquire how it happens that any given economic subject, with his limited knowledge of the facts of life, is able to make a living.   In a thoroughly planned economy, this question need not arise, for we could simply assume that everyone followed instructions from above.   How the planners themselves knew what they were about would afford material for our speculations, but we should be confident from the beginning that the system could be made to work somehow.   On the other hand,

[2] This approach is emphasized in *Business Cycles,* pp. 30ff.

[3] J. S. Mill, *Principles,* Ashley Edition, p. 488.

[4] Since this statement is tautologically true, no examples will be given.

how an unplanned, competitive, exchange economy manages to keep going at all is one of the most fundamental problems that economists have to face.

If we attack our problem by means of a specific example,[5] we see at once what the solution must be. The farmer who grows wheat that later will be made into flour is acting to provide consumers with bread at some time in the more distant future. Neither farmer nor consumer needs to know that the other exists, and neither has to be aware of the complicated links in the chain that connects their activities. All that is necessary is that each should do again what his own experience has already shown to be best for him under conditions that he cannot himself alter. Extending the boundaries of this simple picture to encompass the economy as a whole, we arrive at a stable system of routine activities embedded in a changing society. This circular flow of familiar routine is self-perpetuating, and when interrupted by external events, it tends to re-establish itself. It is capable also of absorbing growth by means of continuous adaptations for which past experience is an adequate guide. Innovation, however, it cannot absorb, for innovation disrupts the routine pattern from within and makes it obsolete.

The superficial similarity between the Schumpeterian circular flow and the stationary state of the classical tradition may be misleading. For the classical economists, the stationary state was the ultimate destination of the economy, and the goal toward which it was moving, steadily and irresistibly, in the grip of forces that were bound to prevail in the long run, temporary interruptions such as "improvement" notwithstanding. In the Schumpeterian System, on the contrary, the circular flow serves precisely to separate innovation from both routine and growth, and to permit the maintenance of a clear distinction between the two classes of phenomena.[6]

With these preliminary considerations in mind, we may now proceed to a discussion of the three principal issues that have arisen in connection with the Schumpeterian circular flow.

---

[5] For this approach see *The Theory of Economic Development,* pp. 5ff. The Walrasian method is also employed in that book later on.

[6] See *Theory of Economic Development,* p. 59n.

The Zero Rate of Interest

That there are possible grounds for suspicion that the interest rate of the circular flow would be positive rather than zero was suggested some twenty years ago by Professor Robbins.[7]   In terms of our preceding sketch, Professor Robbins's objection may be formulated as follows.

Capital exists in the circular flow in the form of equipment and stocks in the hands of private owners.   If output is to be continuously maintained at constant rates, the capitalists must keep these means of further production intact, which means that land and labor must be devoted to the maintenance of capital.   But if the interest rate is zero, there is no net yield to the use of capital, and hence there is no incentive to maintain it.   If, for instance, we consider the owner of a small business which is, under the conditions of the circular flow, just breaking even, why should the owner continue to provide for depreciation out of his revenue, when by not doing so he could increase his own consumption?   In brief, unless there is some positive rate of interest, the capitalists will consume their capital, and the circular flow will collapse.   Professor Schumpeter, it seems, cannot have both fixed amounts of his productive factors and a zero rate of interest in the same circular flow.

To the reader the solution may appear to be obvious, but this has not been a universal impression.   People were not being quite so glib about these matters twenty years ago as they are now, and some economists even today are convinced that the circular flow with a zero interest rate is a logical impossibility.[8]   Our proof that the model is valid is due to Professor Samuelson,[9] and, since the issue is still alive, his solution will bear repetition.

We should begin by observing that the constancy of capital is not

[7] L. Robbins, "On a Certain Ambiguity in the Conception of Stationary Equilibrium," *Economic Journal*, June, 1930.

[8] See L. von Mises, *Human Action*, pp. 527-529.   Compare also E. Heimann, *History of Economic Doctrines*, pp. 227-228, and Gide and Rist, *A History of Economic Doctrines*, 2d English ed., p. 718n.

[9] P. A. Samuelson, "Dynamics, Statics, and the Stationary State," *Review of Economic Statistics*, February, 1943.   Compare the neglected article by D. Warriner, "Schumpeter and the Conception of Static Equilibrium," *Economic Journal*, March, 1931.

assumed in the Schumpeterian circular flow; it is instead deduced from the conditions of the system.   In this world of familiar routine there is no uncertainty regarding the future.   Neither is there time preference unless we introduce it as a special assumption, in which case it may be either positive or negative as we prefer, and there is nothing further to discuss.   This possibility aside, we have only the problem of maximizing utility for an individual over infinite time, his stream of income being given.   Utility being always the same function of income, diminishing marginal utility gives us an even distribution of income through time as the only possible solution. With a zero interest rate, the individual is free to substitute future income for present on even terms, but no substitution could be to his advantage.   Additional present consumption would yield less utility than would have to be sacrificed in reducing future consumption, and similarly for shifts in the opposite direction.   If the owner of a small business failed to provide for depreciation, and increased his current consumption, his total utility over time would be thereby diminished.[10]

We thus conclude that a zero rate of interest is after all quite compatible with the maintenance of capital in the Schumpeterian circular flow.[11]   There remains, however, the related question of the limit approached by the interest rate in the general Schumpeterian System as the effects of innovation are absorbed, and the circular flow tends to be reconstituted.   In other words, is there any limit to the use of capital as its cost approaches zero?

This question has engaged the interest of a large number of

[10] The possibility that some interest payments might be made on consumption loans is not ruled out, but is simply a matter of indifference.   Compare A. H. Hansen, Review of *The Theory of Economic Development, Journal of Political Economy,* August, 1936, p. 561.

[11] In another context, Professor Haberler has called attention to the fact that a zero interest rate would mean that the incomes of capitalists would be independent of the amounts of capital they employed, and that those who used most would thus tend to liquidate part of it and shift to fields in which less was required.   (G. Haberler, "The Interest Rate and Capital Formation," *Capital Formation and Its Elements,* p. 133.   This portion of the paper is included in Swanson and Schmidt, *Economic Stagnation or Progress,* p. 53.)   It will be seen that this is not an objection to the Schumpeterian circular flow, since the capitalist in that model who moved to another field would lose at least a part of his wages of management as zero profits yielded to losses.

economists, and a considerable body of literature has grown up in connection with it.[12] The matter may appear to be of little practical importance, since everyone agrees that such a limit, if it exists, has never been approximated. The problem has, however, implications beyond those visible on the surface, particularly in relation to the whole question of economic maturity and the "stagnation" controversy. Nevertheless, for our purpose it will be sufficient to point out that no analytical solution exists, and that the question is one of objective fact. In the Schumpeterian System, the zero interest rate is, outside the circular flow, only the limit toward which the actual rate is tending as the economy approaches its neighborhoods of long-period equilibrium. What is more important from our standpoint is the fact that a rate other than zero could be substituted as a limit without altering the system in any essential respect. Anyone who holds a theory of interest according to which some positive rate would exist in the circular flow is perfectly free to insert this correction into the Schumpeterian System at whatever points he feels it appropriate to do so.[13]

THE COMPETITIVE ASSUMPTION

The general equilibrium in which the circular flow is conceived to take place is derived from purely competitive assumptions. This has the obvious technical advantages of starting from familiar ground, and of avoiding the difficulties that would arise if an attempt were made to deal with imperfections and monopolistic elements such as are treated in theoretical work nowadays. Though the purely competitive assumption thus makes the establishment of the circular flow much easier than it would otherwise be, this can hardly be regarded as an adequate justification of the procedure. It has, in fact, been asserted that the competitive nature of the circular flow is a serious shortcoming of the whole Schumpeterian System. A direct quotation will best reveal the nature of this objection to the model Professor Schumpeter has chosen:

---

[12] A few of the more important papers are included in *Readings in the Theory of Income Distribution,* and others are listed in the Bibliography in that book.
[13] See *Business Cycles,* pp. 41, 602n., 603n., 634n.

His selection of a general, fully competitive equilibrium model precludes the important study of the effects of change on the market, the
effect of innovation on the degree of competition.   His concept of profits
neglects the possibility of monopolistic surpluses, their effects, their
potential discouragement of innovations, and the effects on aggregate
demand of such surpluses.[14]

One point naturally arises at once.   If the purely competitive assumption is not acceptable, what alternative would there be?   The
theories of monopolistic and imperfect competition are applicable
not to any one or a few clearly defined conditions, but to a great
number of categories and subcategories corresponding to the virtually infinite configurations of reality.   Manifestly, an attempt to
take full account of all these possibilities would be a hopeless undertaking.   A large part of the work even of taxonomy is still in its
early stages,[15] and the area of agreement is not yet impressive.   If
the model were redesigned to include the more familiar cases, it
would still be open to the objection that the inclusion of others
would have made a significant difference.   The purely competitive
assumption is therefore more than a trouble-saving device; it is the
only feasible way to proceed at all.

To this, however, it may properly be objected that feasibility is
a matter of opinion, and that it is more important to get some sort
of monopolistic elements into the circular flow than to achieve analytical perfection at the expense of relevance.   We have so far shown
only that economy and expediency support the use of the purely
competitive assumption, and this is admittedly a weak defense.
Can we do better than this?

---

[14] B. S. Kierstead, *Theory of Economic Change,* p. 98.   Since we shall have
occasion to refer to this book at a number of points in our discussion, a few
remarks concerning it may be made here.   As Professor Kierstead has stated
in his Preface, his book is not a well-developed study, but is rather a collection of loosely related essays.   This may help to explain the fact that,
whereas *Business Cycles* is frequently referred to in the early chapters, the
critical discussion of the Schumpeterian System that appears further on is
inconsistent with the supposition that *Business Cycles* had been read.
Professor Kierstead tells us that in the preparation of these critical pages
he depended largely on the work of one of his students (p. 68), and this
may partly account for the nature of some of the positions arrived at.
[15] Compare J. S. Bain, "Price and Production Policies," *A Survey of Contemporary Economics,* especially pp. 152-162.

The answer is that we can do a great deal better. The really significant reason for insisting on pure competition in the circular flow is that the model is designed to eliminate all effects of innovation from the preliminary formulation in order to make possible a test of the hypothesis that innovation would give rise to monopoly positions in an otherwise purely competitive world. So far from precluding the effective study of the relation of innovation to changes in markets and in the degree of competition, the competitive circular flow opens the door to just this sort of investigation. It will be recalled that the imperfections in question are introduced into the Schumpeterian System with the Second Approximation,[16] and there is hence no question of their being ignored from that point on.

There remains the question of profits, and the complaint that the possibility of monopolistic surpluses and their effects has been neglected. This is a puzzling criticism, for Professor Schumpeter has dealt with these matters at length both in his *Business Cycles* and elsewhere.[17] A great number of passages[18] that would dispel this illusion might easily be quoted; we limit ourselves to the following:

> Such struggles for a share in profits that have been made are, however, less important for our subject than the struggles to conserve the stream of profit itself. Secrecy regarding processes, patents, judicious differentiation of products, advertising, and the like, occasionally also aggression directed against actual and would-be competitors, are instances of a familiar strategy, which in the public, as well as in the professional, mind have done much to veil the source and nature of profits in our sense,

[16] If the objection to the purely competitive model is intended to apply to *The Theory of Economic Development* rather than to *Business Cycles*, we may note that the treatment in the latter is sufficient to show that effective study was not precluded by beginning with the model used in the former.

[17] Again, it is possible that Professor Kierstead is thinking of *The Theory of Economic Development*, and not of *Business Cycles*. His note, however (*Theory of Economic Change*, p. 96), appears to apply to only one point in his discussion, and to one that must be regarded as a matter of opinion. Since readers of Professor Kierstead's book can be expected to assume that the Schumpeterian System as it stands is the object of criticism, we have dealt with the problem from that standpoint. We are, in any event, concerned with the ideas themselves, and their origins are of no more than incidental interest.

[18] Especially in *Capitalism, Socialism, and Democracy*, Part II.

especially because that strategy may be resorted to in other cases as well. We realize at once that these devices are the same as those which play a role in cases of monopolistic competition and that the fact that they are met with in our case is precisely due to the other fact that an enterprise in our sense almost necessarily finds itself in an "imperfect" situation, even if the system be otherwise a perfectly competitive one. This is one of the reasons why we so persistently stress the relation between evolution and imperfection of competition. It follows that profits might, as far as this goes, be also included in the category of monopoloid gains. This, however, would blur the specific character of our case: not every generalization is profitable to the analyst—any more than every innovation is to the innovator. Moreover, profits change their character in the course of such struggles.[19]

THE STRUCTURE OF ECONOMIC SOCIETY

Professor Schumpeter has himself emphasized that his system, even in its first approximation, is strongly institutional in character.[20] His circular flow is a model, not of the economies of all societies, but only of one conforming to his conception of essential capitalist arrangements. In other words, the model is intended to correspond to a particular social pattern existing historically in a definite epoch and in specific areas, and this fact has been frequently stressed by its author. The institutional framework within which the circular flow is conceived to exist has not been the object of much discussion, mainly because most economists readily accept the structure as a tolerable approximation to reality. Though it thus represents what may be thought of as an orthodox vision of the nature of capitalist society, the model is, however, open to objection of a particular type.[21]

From the Marxist standpoint, the capitalist class is inadequately rendered by a scheme in which the owners of capital are without motives for the continued accumulation of wealth. If the model contained a special class of individuals who had complete control over the produced means of production, and if the members of this class enjoyed a social status measured by their relative wealth, then

---

[19] *Business Cycles,* pp. 106-107. The matter is even treated in the short discussion of profits in *The Theory of Economic Development,* p. 152.

[20] See *Business Cycles,* p. 144.

[21] See P. M. Sweezy, "Professor Schumpeter's Theory of Innovation," *Review of Economic Statistics,* February, 1943.

there would be both surpluses and accumulation out of these surpluses in the circular flow. Let us examine this suggestion more carefully.

We may suppose that there exists in capitalist society a distinct class of wealth owners, who by virtue of their control over capital form also a special class of employers apart from landlords and laborers. The laborers, being themselves unable to secure capital and thus to become employers, are incapable of resisting the exploitation inherent in the structure of this society. Thus, the capitalists become the natural beneficiaries of a surplus that we may call profits or interest or a combination of the two, as we prefer. Now, if social prestige is a function of the possession of wealth, such status is a relative matter, and the rational capitalist tends to accumulate without limit. In contrast to the Schumpeterian model, surpluses and accumulation become the causes rather than the effects of change. The introduction of new factor combinations is the means to the survival of the capitalist class, and the vehicle for the individual's remaining a member of that class and advancing within it. In this scheme, therefore, the resistances to innovation are negligible, and there is a continual pressure on the individual capitalist to innovate or take the consequences.

This alternative to the Schumpeterian circular flow has a certain plausibility, and it is not easy to show what is wrong with it. In the circumstances, the proper strategy may be to begin by throwing up a smoke screen behind which to conduct our operations. Professor Schumpeter achieves his stationary economy by abstracting his entrepreneur, and with him innovation, from capitalist society. In the alternative proposal, however, we may doubt that a corresponding procedure is legitimate. The accumulation of capital cannot be abstracted from the model if capitalists with their motives to accumulate are to remain within it. If the capitalists are themselves abstracted in order to obtain a preliminary circular flow, it will be difficult to get them back in again, and to explain how they get hold of all the produced means of production. In the Schumpeterian model there is no such problem, since the entrepreneur is ready to innovate as soon as he appears on the scene, and he needs no assets other than the personal abilities he is taken to possess. These may or may not be more than verbal circumlocutions, but in either event we have so far evaded the main issue, with which we may now deal as follows.

One of the merits of the Schumpeterian System is that it is able to explain how, starting from a society without a definite capitalist class, the process of development, by creating family fortunes, brings a group of hereditary wealth owners into being. What is more important, the model enables us to perceive that the existence of a capitalist class in the Marxist sense is an illusion, and that the titles to membership in this group continually change hands as successful innovation creates new fortunes and destroys old ones. Not only does the Schumpeterian System present a penetrating picture of true capitalist realities, but it also accounts incidentally for the problem of original accumulation which the Marxists themselves are unable to explain. We thus reach the conclusion that the alternative circular flow of Marxist inspiration is unacceptable, and that our analysis disposes of all such claims. Or does it?

Unfortunately, neither our analysis nor any other can possibly prove that Professor Schumpeter is right and the Marxists wrong. The real issue turns on the nature of reality, irreconcilable visions of which no amount of analysis can ever resolve. Those Marxists who are also good theorists are already aware of the arguments we have stated, and they may also be quite ready to go a long way toward accepting the Schumpeterian System.[22] They can never go all the way, however, and remain Marxists. That the Schumpeterian version of capitalist reality is superior to the Marxist[23] seems to us to be obvious. But this is just the difficulty. Those who do not find it obviously superior could never be persuaded that it is superior at all. And, on the basis of their own vision of the world, they would be right.

---

[22] Mr. Sweezy writes: "The rise of new firms and new fortunes, which was such a common feature of the capitalist economy of a generation or two ago, is probably best accounted for along the lines of his theory." ("Professor Schumpeter's Theory of Innovation," p. 96).

[23] For Professor Schumpeter's own views on Marx see *Capitalism, Socialism, and Democracy,* Chapters I-IV. Compare also his "Science and Ideology," and "The Communist Manifesto in Sociology and Economics."

Chapter 6

THE CONCEPT OF INNOVATION

From the standpoint of the economist,[1] production means the combination of quantities of factors. Any such combination may be completely described by means of a production function relating inputs of productive services to output of product per unit of time. At any given time, the production functions in an economy represent the technological possibilities open to firms in the light of the existing state of knowledge. In the circular flow, all the firms in any given industry would not only have identical production functions, but, as we have observed earlier, identical costs as well. A particular productive combination may, of course, be altered within a fixed production function in response to changes in the prices of productive services. In contrast to such adjustments, innovation is defined as "the setting up of a new production function," [2] introducing into the productive system a combination that could not have been made before. Innovation is thus an internal factor from the point of view of the Schumpeterian System, and innovation with its effects and with the response of the economy to these effects is responsible for the process of Economic Evolution.[3]

Some of those critics who in attacking the Schumpeterian structure have penetrated beyond the outposts, have perceived grounds for serious objection to the concept of innovation itself. The major issues that have so far been developed in the literature may be stated as follows:

1. There is first the quite fundamental question of the meaning of the definition. On one side it has been objected that the notion of innovation is so indefinite as to make it uncertain in particular instances whether or not innovation has actually occurred. On the other hand, it has been more than hinted that the definition really amounts to a tautology, in that innovation can be said to start

---

[1] See *Business Cycles,* pp. 38ff.
[2] *Business Cycles,* p. 87.
[3] *Business Cycles,* p. 86.

cycles only because anything that starts cycles is identified as innovation.

2. Beyond the serious charge just mentioned, the concept of innovation has been criticized as being too broad to be useful. Not every new production function, it is contended, constitutes innovation. The concept should be limited to alterations of a narrower type.

3. Whereas some critics find the definition of innovation too broad, others find it too narrow. Unless the concept is extended to cover a greater range of investment outlays, it will remain, it is held, incapable of explaining the historical facts.

4. Aside from matters of definition, it has been asserted that the theory of innovation fails to explain why innovations are introduced in neighborhoods of equilibrium. This question is closely related to the problem of clustering, with which we shall deal in the next chapter. The point to be emphasized is, however, one that falls within the scope of the present discussion.

5. We have, finally, the question of the extent to which innovation is to be regarded as the "single" cause of change. Professor Schumpeter's model, by allowing only one cause of change to operate, has been said to preclude the possibility of developing a comprehensive theory of the process of development.

It is clear that these criticisms, if valid, would damage the Schumpeterian System beyond repair. Any one of them, taken alone, is sufficiently fundamental to merit careful examination, and if it is possible to sustain many of them simultaneously, not much will be left of the concept of innovation on which the model depends. It is even conceivable at this stage of the discussion that all the objections could hold at the same time, for a concept can be, for instance, both too broad and too narrow for the purposes it is intended to serve.

As a preparation for the main encounter it will be well to gather together a little ammunition from the writings of Professor Schumpeter himself. The definition of innovation as "the setting up of a new production function" covers a variety of possible activities; let us see more concretely what these are. The following summary of the specific acts constituting innovation is taken from *The Theory of Economic Development*:[4]

---

[4] P. 66.

This concept covers the following five cases: (1) The introduction of a new good—that is one with which consumers are not yet familiar—or a new quality of a good.   (2) The introduction of a new method of production, that is one not yet tested by experience in the branch of manufacture concerned, which need by no means be founded upon a discovery scientifically new, and can also exist in a new way of handling a commodity commercially.   (3) The opening of a new market, that is a market into which the particular branch of manufacture of the country in question has not previously entered, whether or not this market has existed before.   (4) The conquest of a new source of supply of raw materials or half-manufactured goods, again irrespective of whether this source already exists or whether it has first to be created.   (5) The carrying out of the new organisation of any industry, like the creation of a monopoly position (for example through trustification) or the breaking up of a monopoly position.

In *Business Cycles*,[5] we find another statement to the same effect:

By changes in the methods of supplying commodities we mean a range of events much broader than the phrase covers in its literal acceptance. We include the introduction of new commodities which may even serve as the standard case.   Technological change in the production of commodities already in use, the opening up of new markets or of new sources of supply, Taylorization of work, improved handling of material, the setting up of new business organizations such as department stores—in short, any "doing things differently" in the realm of economic life—all these are instances of what we shall refer to by the term Innovation.   It should be noticed at once that that concept is not synonymous with "invention" (see Chap. I, Sec. B).   Whatever the latter term may mean, it has but a distant relation to ours.   Moreover, it carries misleading associations.

This much provision will serve well enough to establish contact, and more can be brought up as the engagement proceeds.

---

[5] P. 84.   For the relation between innovation and invention see *Business Cycles*, pp. 8-9 and 84-86.   From the standpoint of the Schumpeterian System, invention is not an external factor; it is no factor at all.   It should be observed that this implies nothing concerning such theories of invention as those of Gilfillan, Usher, and others.   It is misleading to think of any theory of invention as a part of the Schumpeterian System.   (See, for example, the reference to Professor Frisch in S. D. Merlin, *The Theory of Fluctuations in Contemporary Economic Thought*, p. 83n.   Professor Frisch, however, did not use the term invention in the work cited.)

THE PROBLEM OF DEFINITION

In order to avoid any possible misunderstanding, we shall state
this issue in the form of a direct quotation. Professor Angell be-
lieves that one of the serious defects of the Schumpeterian System
is that

> . . . the concept of "innovations" turns out to be so fuzzy that its sta-
> tistical and historical usefulness is uncertain. No unequivocal objective
> test or definition of an "innovation" is given. Not *all* "exogeneous"
> disturbances and not even all advances or changes in techniques are
> cycle-starting "innovations." An exogeneous disturbance is an "innova-
> tion" only so far as it does start business cycles. This is dangerously
> close to question begging.[6]

It will be seen that we have two questions to consider here. First,
is Professor Schumpeter's concept of innovation ambiguous, so that
its occurrence in specific instances cannot be clearly established?
Second, is Professor Schumpeter indulging in implicit theorizing[7]
by defining a crucial concept in terms of the phenomenon it is supposed to explain?

With respect to the first question, we shall not argue that the
concept of innovation is so precisely in accord with reality as to
eliminate all ambiguities and make it impossible that borderline
cases should exist. On the contrary, we shall urge quite the opposite. *Natura non facit saltum* may mean a number of things, and
one of them is that the definitions by means of which we establish
our categories correspond imperfectly to the phenomena of the real
world, leaving us always with events for which no neat scheme of
classification will provide. Consider, for instance, the concepts of
"many" and "few," "standardized products" and "differentiated
products," as ordinarily used to characterize market situations.

---

[6] J. W. Angell, *Investment and Business Cycles,* pp. 332-333. Professor Kuznets had a similar impression, and he failed to urge the point only because
the tautology was too obvious to be acceptable as an interpretation of Professor Schumpeter's intentions. See S. S. Kuznets, "Schumpeter's Business
Cycles," *American Economic Review,* June, 1940, p. 263.

[7] Compare W. Leontief, "Implicit Theorizing: A Methodological Criticism
of the Neo-Cambridge School," *Quarterly Journal of Economics,* February,
1937, pp. 340-346, for some good examples of the use of this technique.

Whether we define innovation in terms of the production function, or in terms of the business man's horizon,[8] or in terms of money cost,[9] marginal difficulties are bound to arise when we look for actual cases to fit our conceptual scheme. If we attempt to follow any business man as he deals with the daily problems that confront him, we realize that the dividing line between innovation and ordinary routine cannot be clearly drawn. It is easy enough to say that some changes in factor combinations lie within a given production function, and that others imply the setting up of a new one, but except in spectacular instances who can tell which is which?[10] If we look to Professor Schumpeter himself for help on these matters, we find that, far from giving us comfort, he has gone quite out of his way to insist that innovation shall not be taken to mean great changes, and to supply examples of innovations so modest as to be nearly invisible.[11] Can it be that he failed to realize what he was doing to his theoretical structure, and thus deprived it of adequate support? Or, did he recognize the existence of a problem, and make some attempt to deal with it?

The answer is clear enough. As we saw in Chapter 2, the difficulty is resolved in the construction of the Pure Model. When it becomes necessary to transfer the concept of innovation from the realm of speculative reasoning to a model of the capitalist process, ambiguities are left to one side by introducing the qualification that all innovations are to be identified with the founding of new firms and the rise of new men to business leadership.[12] From this point on there can therefore be no question of the nature of a historical or statistical test of innovating activity. Either new things are done by new firms or they are not, and whether the facts are easy or difficult to establish, we know what objective facts will prove the presence or absence of innovation. Naturally, something must be sacrificed to achieve this end. Some innovation, particularly of the type that takes effect within the corporate shell of the modern large-scale enterprise, is excluded from the model, and must be dealt with separately on the merits of each individual case. Professor Schum-

---

[8] See *Business Cycles,* p. 40.
[9] See *Business Cycles,* pp. 88-89.
[10] Compare D. M. Wright, *The Economics of Disturbance,* p. 34.
[11] See *Business Cycles,* p. 92. In this example, even the tailor himself might well be in doubt as to whether or not he was innovating.
[12] See *Business Cycles,* pp. 93-96.

peter, faced with the choice, has deliberately limited the application of his schema to the historical epoch prior to what he refers to as "Trustified Capitalism," and has cautioned against its use in other periods except as justified by careful investigation.[13]

It should by now be evident that the second charge can be no better sustained than the first. There is no circularity in the definition of innovation, and the phenomenon can be identified independently of the effects it tends to produce. We shall return to this point in our discussion of the impact of innovation, but another word or two may be inserted here.

Innovation is the function of a sociological type of individuals known as entrepreneurs.[14] These men possess in more than ordinary degree the qualities of leadership, which finds expression in capitalist society primarily in the business sphere. The Pure Model is designed to show how the elimination of entrepreneurs from the economy removes the source of change, leaving a circular flow of activity, and how the reintroduction of the entrepreneur gives rise to cycles of economic development. Entrepreneurs, from whatever strata of society they may come, are thus an objectively defined class of individuals, and their existence is not simply deduced from what they do. Starting from equilibrium, innovation will start a business cycle, but as we shall see later on it is by no means true that all innovations start cycles. This they would, of course, have to do if the concept were really question begging.

Is the Concept of Innovation Too Broad?

In discussing this criticism, we again find it convenient to begin with a quotation. Concerning the "setting up of a new production function," Professor Lange has written:

> This definition, however, is too wide. A large (possibly even infinite) number of ways always exists in which production functions can be

---

[13] See *Business Cycles*, p. 145. The point was made earlier in "The Instability of Capitalism," *Economic Journal*, September, 1928, pp. 384-386.
[14] See P. M. Sweezy, "Professor Schumpeter's Theory of Innovation," *Review of Economic Statistics*, February, 1943, pp. 93-96. Mr. Sweezy writes (p. 94): . . . "unlike many of his critics, I have no fault to find with the logic of Professor Schumpeter's argument; on the contrary, it appears to me indisputable that on its own assumptions his theory of the mechanism of economic change is unassailable."

changed. But an innovation appears only when there is a possibility of such a change, which increases the (discounted) maximum effective profit the firm is able to make. All other possible changes are disregarded by the firms.[15]

This suggestion for refining the concept of innovation appears to have considerable merit, and for some purposes[16] it may represent an improvement in definition. In the Schumpeterian System, however, it is by no means acceptable.

As we have seen, Professor Schumpeter in building his Pure Model has to restrict his concept in order to fit it for that purpose. In so doing, the phenomenon of innovation within already existing firms has to be ignored in the model proper, while attention is concentrated on the founding of new firms and the rise of new men to leadership. The choice is made on the ground that it focuses the analysis on the outstanding features of a particular historical period, and thus brings the model into closer conformity with the data of this era than would be possible if a different concept of innovation were employed. Professor Lange's proposal would, on the other hand, confine the concept to just those phenomena that the Schumpeterian definition is intended to exclude. It is true that when the new production function is first identified with innovation there is no attempt at a detailed explanation of the reasons why the narrower alternative will not do. As the System is developed, however, it becomes evident that less generality at the outset would have made it impossible to construct the model required.

We must therefore conclude that the concept of innovation in the Schumpeterian System is not too broad for the purposes it has to serve, and that Professor Lange's alternative would reduce the usefulness of the model to negligible proportions.

Is the Concept of Innovation Too Narrow?

Corresponding to the two aspects of the Schumpeterian concept of innovation, we have two types of objection to it. Since the pre-

---

15 O. Lange, "A Note on Innovations," *Review of Economic Statistics,* February, 1943, p. 21n.
16 Compare, for instance, the use made of a similar concept in *Cost Behavior and Price Policy,* especially Chapter VII.

liminary definition is subsequently refined in terms of new firms and men, the concept may be attacked in either its pure form or the restricted form later introduced. As we have seen, the failure to appreciate the significance of this distinction has been a source of some confusion. We now observe that those critics who find the concept of innovation too narrow have not made it clear to which formulation they are objecting. For purposes of the following discussion we shall therefore assume that it is the more limited concept of which they complain, and let our results apply to the other *a fortiori*.

We have two criticisms to consider—one superficial and the other of more importance. We begin with the former, which may be quickly disposed of.

Professor Kierstead writes:

> The incentive to innovation is the possibility of profit, which cannot be earned in the stationary society. For Professor Schumpeter profit is tied by definition to innovation. It is the extra gain an entrepreneur can acquire by lowering his costs below his competitors. This is the function of entrepreneurship. But, in the model, costs can only be lowered below the competitive level by the introduction of some productive technique previously unused, in other words, by an innovation. Thus, for Professor Schumpeter, profits are a dynamic phenomenon only. They are possible only in a dynamic society, and this possibility is the incentive to development. This emphasis, we might note, implies that Professor Schumpeter, in spite of his recognition that an innovation may take the form of the introduction of a new good, in fact always thinks of it as the introduction of new—and less costly ways—of making old goods.[17]

Since Professor Kierstead himself remarks that restricting the concept of innovation to cost-reducing changes is not a serious matter, and that the analysis may easily be extended to cover the introduction of new goods, we shall merely point out that the criticism is not only unimportant but incorrect as well. The quotation from *Business Cycles* reproduced earlier in this chapter is sufficient to show that the introduction of a new good may be taken as the standard case, and this is amply supported by the whole treatment. Even if we go back to the analysis of 1911, and confine our attention to

---

[17] B. S. Kierstead, *Theory of Economic Change,* p. 96.

that, we find a detailed discussion of all types of innovation in connection with the question of entrepreneurial profit.[18]

Turning to a more important objection, we find Professor Rostow speaking from the standpoint of the economic historian. He raises a number of points, some of which may be more conveniently considered elsewhere, but two of which bear on the present issue. In listing his criticisms[19] of the Schumpeterian System, Professor Rostow writes:

> Third, the scale and consequences of innovations, in the technical sense in which Schumpeter uses the term, are demonstrably inadequate to explain the central phenomena of several of the trend periods, if they are examined in detail; e. g. the innovations of the Industrial Revolution, during the French wars, and the role of electricity and the automobile in the fifteen years before 1914.
>
> Fourth, if the concept of innovations is broadened until it approximates to what are called here outlays for purposes other than consumption, or investment outlays, the theory would have to be broadened to include the timing and character of wars, as well as other more or less adventitious events, without which a satisfactory historical explanation of these years is impossible.[20]

Professor Rostow would presumably agree that his fourth point is subordinate to his third, and that the concept of innovations need be broadened only if it is too narrow as it stands. The third point, then, poses the real issue, and it is one of great significance.

If we examine Professor Rostow's statement with some care, we see immediately that its validity depends entirely on what the "central phenomena" of the periods in question are supposed to be. Professor Schumpeter regards the central phenomena of the capitalist era as those of the process of economic evolution arising out of innovation with all its effects, including the responses made by the entire economy. His model is expressly designed to explain these phenomena, and the only way to show that it does not is to prove

---

[18] See *The Theory of Economic Development,* Chapter IV. The introduction of new goods is discussed on pp. 134-136.

[19] His first is that there are serious ambiguities concerning just what is supposed to fluctuate in the Kondratieffs; his second is that the recurrence and comparatively constant periodicity of the long cycles are not explained. The two points discussed in the text above complete the list. We shall undertake to deal with problems of the long waves in Chapter 10.

[20] W. W. Rostow, *British Economy of the Nineteenth Century,* p. 29.

that there is something fundamentally wrong with the whole Schum-peterian System.   Otherwise, it is simply impossible to say that the concept of innovation is "demonstrably inadequate" to explain these central phenomena.

If, on the other hand, the central phenomena are taken to be quite different from those in which Professor Schumpeter is inter-ested, it requires no demonstration to show that his model does not explain them satisfactorily.

Professor Rostow, then, is questioning the adequacy of the Schum-peterian System from the standpoint of an economic historian who is faced with the problem of dealing with data that fall outside the confines of the model.   To this we may reply that the model fully provides for the recognition and separate treatment of external fac-tors, and that there is no reason why economic historians should refuse to accept the distinction and use it in their own work.   In-deed, it must often appear to economists that historians as a group are singularly indisposed to make use of anything but the crudest tools of the theorist, and that those who do rely much on theory learned theirs too long ago.   Certainly the economic historian can-not even collect facts without some preconceptions concerning what is meaningful and what is not, and if he is reluctant to rely on good theory he is likely to end by accepting bad.   If this were all that needed saying, things would be easier than they are.   There is, however, something more.

To the historian it must doubtless seem that the theorist is alto-gether too eager to force the facts into a mold, and too ready to throw away any that cannot be jammed in.   The student of history is bound to be impressed with the enormous variety of events that he encounters, and to be acutely concious of the losses involved in any attempt to impose patterns of uniformity on reality.   "Nature's ac-tion is complex: and nothing is gained in the long run by pretending that it is simple, and trying to describe it in a series of elementary propositions." [21]   These words, it is true, were written by an econo-mist, but he also knew something about history, and therefore real-ized how tentative all attempts at generalization must be.

In the light of all this, what are we to conclude about the Schum-

---

[21] A. Marshall, *Principles of Economics*, Preface to the first edition.   For a historian's statement see W. O. Henderson, "Trade Cycles in the 19th Cen-tury," *History*, July, 1933, p. 153.

peterian System as an engine for historical analysis? Does it or does it not fit the needs of the historian better than other available schemes? The answer is that nobody knows. We are dealing with a problem similar, in some respects, to that raised by the Marxist alternative. What is reality? What are the central phenomena in it? What are we trying to explain? Economists and historians of the orthodox faith should be able to agree more nearly on these matters with one another than with their brethren of the Marxist creed. Nevertheless, there is room for differences of opinion, and there is no reason why we should insist that it be otherwise. If everyone were agreed on the nature of reality, and content with the existing explanations of it, the prospects for further progress would be dark indeed.

Our conclusion, with which we believe Professor Rostow agrees,[22] is that the economic historian should regard the Schumpeterian System as a significant achievement in the reconciliation of theory and history—significant in the sense that it is deserving of the most thorough study and testing in order to determine the extent to which it illuminates the course of history.

"Why Innovations Are Innovated"

The question of why innovations should be introduced in neighborhoods of equilibrium is closely allied with the question of clustering, with which the next chapter is concerned. The former issue, however, arises in connection not so much with the reasons for the clustering of innovations as with the assumption that they will be introduced at all. To quote Professor Angell:

Second, no explanation is given of why a depression equilibrium following the adjustment to one wave of innovations should be followed by, or should give rise to, another wave—that is, to speak loosely, of why innovations are innovated. In other words, if business cycles are regarded as self-generating (the view adopted in the present study), no explanation of the process of self-generation is given; whereas if they are regarded as the result of a series of innovations which act as cycle starters, no explanation of the appearance of these cycle starters themselves is given.[23]

---

[22] Our conclusion is at least consistent with his position. Compare *British Economy*, p. 30.
[23] *Investment and Business Cycles*, p. 333.

The suggestion that cycles are regarded as self-generating in the Schumpeterian System is not meant to be taken seriously, since this approach was repudiated too vigorously to admit of any doubt.[24] The question at issue, therefore, is that of why innovations are innovated in equilibrium neighborhoods. We must naturally assume that the phrase "depression equilibrium" is intended to refer to such neighborhoods, for if it meant depression literally, the answer would simply be that innovations are not supposed to be concentrated in depressions, and there would be nothing more to discuss.

In dealing with the problem of definition, we have already seen that the introduction of innovation into the original circular flow presents no difficulties. We have now to show that the same is true when the model is subsequently developed to encompass a series of successive cycles. This may be done as follows:

We have previously observed that the Schumpeterian System is strongly institutional in character. It assumes not only private property and private initiative but a definite type of both of them.[25] Similarly, not merely money and banks are postulated, but it is assumed that the moral code and business tradition of bankers will correspond to the realities of a definite historical epoch. Still more important for the present problem, a business spirit and scheme of motivation such as has characterized capitalist society in the past is taken to exist. In other words, the presence of entrepreneurs within the Schumpeterian System is assured.

We are now entitled to claim that innovation in equilibrium neighborhoods is assured also. If innovation failed to appear, the capitalist process would come to an end. In the past, entrepreneurs have innovated, and recovery has been succeeded by prosperity. In the future, we have no reason to believe that this will go on happening forever. On the contrary, there are good reasons for believing that it will not.[26] The Schumpeterian System, however,

---

24 See *Business Cycles*, p. 157.
25 For Professor Schumpeter's list of these assumptions, see *Business Cycles*, pp. 144-145. Most of them are clearly implicit in the whole treatment.
26 See especially the discussion in *Business Cycles*, pp. 1011-1050; Chapters XI-XIV of *Capitalism, Socialism, and Democracy;* and the new Chapter XXVIII in the 1947 edition of the latter. Compare also Professor Schumpeter's paper, "Capitalism in the Postwar World," in *Postwar Economic Problems*.

is rooted in history, and within the system we may be sure that innovations are innovated.

*

INNOVATION AS A "SINGLE CAUSE"

It has been held that the concept of innovation as a single cause of change is a weakness of the Schumpeterian System, and that the model, by permitting only this one cause to operate, makes it impossible to develop a comprehensive theory of economic change. In Professor Kierstead's words:

> The more recent writings of Professor Alvin Hansen, with a pessimistic tone resembling in some ways that of Karl Marx, require of us a critical approach to Professor Schumpeter's system. Professor Hansen believes that there are three given and external causes of economic change, which act more or less independently. Professor Schumpeter does not explicitly deny these other causes. On the contrary, he insists on the complexity of the causes of change. But he does select a model for analysis in which only one cause is allowed to operate. We do not intend to be understood that this is not valuable analysis, and a perfectly proper use of limitation and selection. It is, however, distinctly limiting, and precludes the possibility of a comprehensive theory of economic change. Professor Schumpeter's general optimism would be dimmed, perhaps, by a study of other models, in which other causes present in the real world, were allowed to operate.[27]

Is this a valid criticism? We do not believe it is. Professor Hansen has enumerated the three causes of change in question as follows:

> . . . the constituent elements of economic progress are: (a) inventions, (b) the discovery and development of new territory and new resources, and (c) the growth of population. Each of these in turn, severally and in combination, has opened investment outlets and caused a rapid growth of capital formation.[28]

Reference to the specific activities constituting innovation summarized near the beginning of this chapter will show that the concept includes the development of new resources and new markets,

---

[27] B. S. Kierstead, *Theory of Economic Change*, p. 97.
[28] A. H. Hansen, *Fiscal Policy and Business Cycles*, p. 352. Compare *Theory of Economic Change*, p. 161n. The degree of independence is, in Professor Hansen's opinion, less rather than more.

and thus brings the phenomena related to territorial expansion within the scope of the analysis. Inventions, of course, are also included to the extent that anything comes of them in the economic sphere. The issue therefore reduces to the question of population, and to whether or not the exclusion of population changes from the model precludes the possibility of a comprehensive theory of change.

Let us see why population changes were not included in the model to begin with. To quote Professor Schumpeter:

> Increase in productive resources might at first sight appear to be the obvious prime mover in the process of internal economic change. Physical environment being taken as constant (opening up of new countries enters as we have seen into a different category), that increase resolves itself into increase of population and the increase of the stock of producers' goods. Neither can, of course, be treated as an independent variable; both are at the same time effects of economic changes and conditions of other economic changes. Our reason for listing variations in population among external factors was that there is no unique relation between them and variations in the flow of commodities. Hence, it seemed convenient for our purpose, although it would be inadequate for others, to look upon an increase in population as an environmental change conditioning certain phenomena. Moreover, it could be demonstrated by familiar cases (India and China) that mere increase in population does not *bring about* any of those phenomena which presuppose either a certain density or a certain rate of increase in population except a fall in real income per head. Finally, it occurs so continuously as to be capable of current absorption. Short-time variations in marriage rates are obviously the reflex of business fluctuations and do not cause them.[29]

The reasons, then, for excluding population changes are partly factual and partly a matter of convenience for the purpose at hand.[30] To the extent that the justification is factual, the population element must naturally be kept out, and an attempt to insert it would lead to abortive results. On the other hand, there would appear to be no reason why such aspects of population growth as have been excluded from the model on grounds of convenience alone should not be made a part of an expanded model if anyone cares

---

[29] *Business Cycles,* p. 74.
[30] See *Business Cycles,* p. 10.

to take the trouble to do so.[31]   In brief, there is nothing about the Schumpeterian System that precludes such a possibility, and the model provides an excellent basis for just this sort of treatment.

---

[31] This might even serve to describe what Professor Kierstead has done. His results (*Theory of Economic Change,* pp. 180-182) are not generally incompatible with such a supposition, though an exception must be made for his conclusion on the monopoly question.

Chapter 7

THE CLUSTERING OF INNOVATIONS

Once an innovation has been successfully introduced into the economy it tends to be followed by attempts at imitation and improvement. Some entrepreneurs enter the innovating area in the hope of making profits, and their successes smooth the path for others to follow. The result of this sequence of events is the phenomenon known as the clustering of innovations.

In the Schumpeterian System, the clustering of innovations in neighborhoods of equilibrium is relied upon to convert recovery into prosperity, and if the innovating activity were not renewed the economy would drift toward a stationary state very different from capitalist society. We observed in the previous chapter that there is no difficulty in accounting for the emergence of innovation as long as the existence of capitalism itself is assumed. The issue now to be dealt with is that of the explanation of clustering. Does the model account satisfactorily for this phenomenon, or is there something wrong with this aspect of the analysis?

We may observe at the outset that our problem is a theoretical one, and does not involve us in matters of empirical fact. It is not therefore open to us to fall back on statistical data that support the statement that the rise of new firms tends to concentrate in historical equilibrium neighborhoods. The truth of this statement is not being denied. What is questioned is that the Schumpeterian System explains this course of events, and some critics are convinced that it does not, and that the whole model must be rejected for that reason.

The principal objections raised against the explanation of clustering are as follows:

1. First, there is the criticism that there can be clustering of innovations only if there is discontinuity over time in the distribution of entrepreneurial ability. Since no cyclical fluctuations in such ability are postulated, it is therefore held that the clustering

phenomenon lacks a rationale and cannot be accounted for by the theory.

2. Second, it is objected that in supposing innovations to be concentrated in equilibrium neighborhoods, Professor Schumpeter has relied too heavily on the principle of increasing risk, and that he has failed to realize that a greater risk of failure in the boom is offset by increasing aggregate profits.

3. Third, it is said that the slump, like the boom, contains elements strongly favorable to innovation, and that there is thus as much *a priori* justification for locating the clustering here as for placing it anywhere else.

Let us proceed to consider these objections in order. We shall again make considerable use of direct quotation, since on these issues the critics have formulated their statements concisely.

CYCLES IN ENTREPRENEURIAL ABILITY?

Professor Kuznets has expressed his belief that the theory of clustering depends upon the existence of cycles of entrepreneurial ability. His position is as follows:

> The theory definitely calls for discontinuity *over time* in the operation of entrepreneurial ability. But such discontinuity cannot be derived from a distribution of entrepreneurial ability *at any given moment of time,* except on one assumption—namely, that the ability called for is so scarce that it may be completely absent during some periods of time while present at others. But this implies cycles in the supply of entrepreneurial ability, whether the supply be conceived in terms of individuals or of phases in the life of various individuals. I am not sure that Professor Schumpeter would view this assumption as valid.[1]

Unless the assumption of discontinuity over time in the supply of entrepreneurial ability is made, the phenomenon of clustering cannot, on this view, be accounted for:

> Given an infinite supply of possible innovations (inventions and other new combinations), why need entrepreneurial genius defer the next pioneering step until his preceding one has been so imitated and expanded that the upsetting of the equilibrium stops even him in his

---

[1] S. S. Kuznets, "Schumpeter's Business Cycles," *American Economic Review,* June, 1940, p. 263.

tracks? If imitators are ready to follow as soon as the entrepreneurial genius has proved that the innovation is successful, the disturbance of equilibrium at that time is certainly not sufficient to bar this genius from turning to new feats and thus initiating an uprush in another industry. Why should we not conceive these applications of high entrepreneurial ability, whether represented by one man or several, as flowing in a continuous stream, a stream magnified in a constant proportion by the efforts of the imitators? [2]

Professor Kuznets has made it clear that he means his objection to apply strictly to the Pure Model of the Schumpeterian System, and our discussion will therefore be confined to that scheme. We should note before continuing that a possible source of the difficulty lies in the repeated characterization of the entrepreneur as a "genius." If we choose to endow entrepreneurs with superhuman capacities, we may naturally have trouble in seeing why they cannot do many things not postulated in the model. Professor Schumpeter, however, has been particularly concerned to guard against this misconception. He writes, for example:

> This ability to decide in favor of untried possibilities or to choose not only between tried but also between tried and untried ones, may, however, be distributed in the population according to the Gaussian—though more plausibly a skew—law, and should not be thought of as confined to a few exceptional cases.[3]

And again:

> . . . these people are by no means looked upon as particularly rare birds. All we postulate is that that ability is distributed as unequally as others are and all we hold is that this fact has an important influence on the mechanism of economic change . . .[4]

In the light of these statements our problem is appreciably diminished. There can now be no mystery concerning the failure of a first entrepreneur to turn from one success to another, and thus maintain a continuous flow of innovations and prosperity. It will be recalled that the establishment of a new enterprise is explicitly

---

[2] S. S. Kuznets, "Schumpeter's Business Cycles," pp. 262-263.
[3] *Business Cycles*, p. 99.
[4] *Business Cycles*, p. 130.

assumed to occupy a considerable length of time, and it is clear that the entrepreneur must stick with his firm for some interval during which he secures his reward. There are, of course, practical devices for reducing this interval to a minimum, but the mere business of promotion is time consuming, and by the time success is assured the prosperity phase will be well advanced. Since the entrepreneur is by no means a genius, there is no reason to imagine that he makes a business of innovation. His object is more properly to be regarded as the founding of a firm, for which innovation is a necessary incident.[5] Thus, innovation need not be continuous simply because entrepreneurial ability is continuously present in the system, and the phenomenon of clustering is independent of any such assumption.

If clustering does not require discontinuity in the appearance of entrepreneurial ability, how is it to be explained? A fundamental element in the explanation is the fact that equilibrium conditions are ideally suited to the introduction of innovations. Indeed, within the confines of the Pure Model to which our problem is now limited, this is virtually the entire explanation.[6]

Why is innovating activity most favored by equilibrium? A comparison of the difficulties and risks of innovation at different stages of the two-phase cycle shows a heavy balance in favor of this situation. The stability of business conditions, as well as the complete absence of profits, is more conducive to innovation than any other stage of the cycle could be. Since the risk of failure is at a minimum, and the pressure to innovate at a maximum, we should expect that innovating activity, under capitalist arrangements, would be extraordinarily great.

Innovation must obviously start off in some definite direction, which means that it is likely to be confined to one or a few fields as prosperity develops. The first success breaks down resistances and smooths the path for others, at the same time affording clear evidence of profit opportunities that were before open to doubt. Recalling the function of bankers in the process, we may further observe that they will be much readier to finance ventures in proven

---

[5] Compare *Theory of Economic Development*, p. 77.
[6] See *Theory of Economic Development*, Chapter VI, especially pp. 214ff. Earlier formulations had been questioned in the German literature, and the discussion in these pages adequately covers the critical points.

fields than in those as yet untested. There is thus no difficulty in accounting for the concentration of innovation in periods of equilibrium, and it needs no extended argument to show that in no other part of a two-phase cycle can the same sort of phenomenon be expected. In place of further discussion, we shall therefore close our treatment of this issue with a quotation from Professor Lange:

> The standard criticism which has been raised against Professor Schumpeter's theory of the business cycle is concerned with the "clustering" of innovations at certain periods of time. The explanation sought by the critics was either in terms of the social psychology of innovations, i.e., that one successful innovation encourages others (a point which Professor Schumpeter himself makes, cf. Vol. i, p. 100, which, however, is not of decisive importance for the theory), or in terms of a clustering in time of technological inventions. These explanations being refuted, the theory was easily rejected. But all this is quite irrelevant. Professor Schumpeter's theory does not rest upon either of these points. The clustering is a consequence of the changing risk of failure. Whatever the time shape of the supply of new inventions, new plans of organization, etc., or of entrepreneurial skill, the actual introduction of innovations will be "bunched" at periods of neighborhood of equilibrium when the risk of failure is the smallest; and as an intensification of the rate of innovation disequilibrates the economy and increases the risk of failure, this rate must slacken again. Thus we can dismiss the standard criticism; the clustering is explained quite satisfactorily in Professor Schumpeter's theory.[7]

THE EFFECT OF WINDFALL GAINS

When we leave the confines of the Pure Model and go on to the Second Approximation, the problem of clustering arises in another

---

[7] O. Lange, Review of Schumpeter's *Business Cycles, Review of Economic Statistics,* November, 1941, p. 192. Professor Kuznets ("Schumpeter's Business Cycles," pp. 263-264) suggested that the clustering of innovations might rest on a clustering of technological inventions. We have not dealt with this point separately, since it is adequately disposed of by the argument in the text. Professor Hansen has frequently remarked upon the discontinuity of emergence of important new industries (see, for examples, *Fiscal Policy and Business Cycles,* Chapters I and XVII), and much criticism of his statements has been based on the ground that technological change is unpredictable, not directly related to economic fluctuations, and so on. See, for instances, G. Terborgh, *The Bogey of Economic Maturity,* Chapter VII; and M. V. Jones, *Secular Trends and Idle Resources,* Chapter II. Since Professor Hansen was following Schumpeterian conceptions, it is apparent that the objections are irrelevant.

form.   It is quite possible to agree that the concentration of innovations is adequately accounted for in the preliminary model, and still to insist that the explanation will not hold for the system in its final form.   Mr. Rothbarth put the matter as follows:

> The chief weakness of the theory appears to consist in its excessive reliance on the influence upon the process of innovation of such variations in risk as are due to the trade cycle itself.   Why does the process of innovation start in a certain period?   Because the system is in the neighborhood of equilibrium and the risk of failure is consequently small.   Why does innovation slacken?   Because at a certain stage of the boom, owing to the impact of innovation on the economic system, the risk of failure increases.   But, it may be argued, innovation is a risky business in any case and will only be undertaken if the prospective profits far exceed "normal profits."   This being so, will the cyclical variation in risk be sufficiently large to make a great impression on the rate of innovation?   As the system departs from equilibrium, risks of failure may increase, but so do aggregate profits—a fact neglected by Professor Schumpeter because he never systematically analyses the effect of the removal of his first-approximation-assumption of full employment.[8]

The question, then, is whether or not the windfall gains of boom conditions compensate for the increasing risk of founding a new firm. If they do, then it follows that innovation should continue as actively during the boom as in the equilibrium neighborhoods, and the earlier account of clustering will no longer hold.

Put thus baldly, the question appears to answer itself.   Since the entrepreneurs who innovate do not spring full-armed from the brow of Professor Schumpeter, but are business men of some experience and connections, why should the windfall gains of established enterprises furnish a special inducement to them to undertake projects of dubious promise?   By staying where they are, they are assured of extraordinary returns; if they found new firms, they may get nothing. Even if potential entrepreneurs are not already in a position to reap large windfalls, speculation is clearly preferable to innovation. In brief, boom conditions are unfavorable to innovation, and favorable to a continuation of the activities that are proven sources of gain.   It is even probable that routine business, to say nothing of innovation, will be neglected as speculative opportunities multiply.

---

[8] E. Rothbarth, Review of Schumpeter's *Business Cycles, Economic Journal,* June-September, 1942, p. 226.

The Effect of Depression

We have seen that the boom conditions introduced in the Second Approximation tend to reinforce, rather than to counteract, the primary tendencies.We have now to consider the question of the slump. Since depression is altogether excluded from the preliminary model, the problem arises only in connection with the subsequent formulation, and must be dealt with in that context. Like the previous question, this one was raised by Mr. Rothbarth, who wrote as follows:

> It is, in fact, possible that the rate of innovation should increase during the slump as the decline of profits sharpens the wits of the "old firms." It seems very difficult to hold any *a priori* theory as to which phase of the trade cycle is most conducive either to the initiation or the rapid diffusion of innovation. The most plausible hypothesis appears to be that extreme prosperity and extreme depression are on the whole less conducive to innovation than mild prosperity and mild slump.[9]

This statement clearly contains more than a grain of truth, and it would be unwise to argue that it is wrong. Must we then agree that Professor Schumpeter has overlooked a fundamental point in developing his analysis, and that his system is thereby invalidated? Not at all. We have only to read Mr. Rothbarth's words with some care to see at once that a false issue is being raised, and that the concept of innovation is being used in two different senses.

The innovation of mild prosperity is the innovation of the Schumpeterian System, clustered about an equilibrium neighborhood, and characterized by the founding of new firms to give effect to new possibilities. So far, so good.

The innovation of the slump is a horse of another color. He is, however, no stranger to the Schumpeterian stable, but finds himself quite at home there. As soon as we shift our concept of innovation, and make it apply to the reactions of existing firms instead of to the starting of new ones, we create unnecessary difficulties by playing with words. The adjustments made by old firms to the conditions of depression are an important part of the Schumpeterian System. We have seen why the term innovation was not used to denote these phenomena, and we now have an example of the confusion that arises when the original distinction is not preserved.

---

[9] E. Rothbarth, *Economic Journal*, June-September, 1942, p. 227.

Chapter 8

THE IMPACT OF INNOVATION

In examining the impact of innovation on the capitalist economy we are confronted with some of the most fundamental questions with which economists have to deal. To undertake any considerable discussion of these matters would take us far beyond the immediate issues that are within the scope of this study. At the same time, we must recognize that the immediate issues cannot be adequately treated without some reference to the far-reaching problems out of which they arise. There is no good way out of this dilemma, but the least objectionable for our purposes appears to be to stray from our main course to the least possible extent. This means that the broader implications of the points at issue will be recognized in passing, but that our attention will remain focused on the Schumpeterian System and the effect of specific criticisms upon it.

We shall be concerned with four main questions:

1. What is the relation of the impact of innovation to the theory of employment? It has been said that the outstanding weakness of the Schumpeterian System is its failure to provide a theory of employment comparable to that furnished in Keynes's *General Theory*. Is this a valid objection?

2. What is the impact of innovation on the character of competition? Professor Schumpeter is said to have imputed the past achievements of capitalist enterprise to monopolistic restrictions in contrast to free competition. Is this a correct interpretation of his position?

3. How is innovation related to investment opportunity? It has been said that the Schumpeterian System overstresses the competitive aspects of innovation to the comparative neglect of the possible effects of innovation in creating new opportunities for investment.

4. How is the impact of innovation related to the nature of business cycles? The Schumpeterian System has been criticized on the ground that it is remote from statistical fact, and that there is no

way to link the model to statistical reality. Is this true? If so, what implications has this for the study of cycles?

We proceed at once to a discussion of these four questions.

INNOVATION AND THE THEORY OF EMPLOYMENT

Professor Lange, in his review of *Business Cycles*, rejected what he referred to as the "standard criticism" of the Schumpeterian System, and then went on to remark:

> The real weakness of his theory appears to be . . . the lack of an adequate theory of employment (in the sense of Mr. Keynes) to serve as a basis for the theory of the business cycle.
> The fluctuation of the level of employment (and of the degree of utilization of resources) is our primary empirical datum about the business cycle. As long as it is not explicitly connected with the theory and assigned in it its due role, Professor Schumpeter's theory must be regarded, at least, as incomplete.[1]

We begin by observing that Professor Lange does not mean to say that the Schumpeterian System takes no account of unemployment. It would be easy to show that a highly suggestive analysis has been made in *Business Cycles*,[2] and this is a fact of which Professor Lange is well aware. As the reference to Keynes indicates, the point is that Professor Schumpeter has not developed a model in which the level of employment is uniquely determined by the functional relationships postulated for the system. We must agree immediately that this is correct. But is it a valid criticism of the Schumpeterian System? Quite the opposite.

We must not permit the brilliance of the Keynesian achievement to blind us to the fact that the *General Theory* presents a theory of employment in only a peculiar sense of that term. As everyone knows, it was only by holding all production functions rigidly fixed that Keynes was able to arrive at a determinate level of employment at all. One innovation in the Keynesian model would spell goodbye to the whole structure. Without going into the merits of the *General Theory* for other purposes, we are entitled to claim that it furnishes the example we want in order to show on what a theory of

---

[1] O. Lange, *Review of Economic Statistics*, November, 1941, p. 192.
[2] Pp. 509-519.

employment must depend. In a world in which innovation is important, changing production functions will be continually destroying the link between employment and output, and it is on such a world that Professor Schumpeter's model is focused. As he has himself written:

> We have seen that there is no unique or simple relation between employment (number of hours worked per week) and output, and that the latter is not proportional to, or measured by, the former. This is a consequence of the very nature of economic evolution and becomes obvious as soon as some of the conditions for proportionality are stated: production functions would have to be invariant in time and relative prices of factors would have to be constant. Neither can possibly be fulfilled for any length of time, such as the period of a Juglar. But both may be fulfilled approximately in the very short run, for which, moreover, the second need not always be fulfilled, because adaptation to change in relative prices of factors may not be possible within it. This very short run may extend, though it cannot be relied on to do so, to the span of a Kitchin, which will, therefore, in this respect, present a picture different from that of the longer cycles. It should also be observed that total employment or unemployment would in any case be unsatisfactory as an index of business situations, even if figures were as exact as they are rough, and even if it were possible to correct them for all the circumstances that change their significance in time (attitude of workmen to unemployment and to relief, geographical and industrial mobility, length of working day, and so on). For variation in total employment or unemployment is the net result of what actually goes on in industrial regions and trades—let alone concerns—and tends to hide differences, which from our standpoint often are what matters most. This may be illustrated by the case of seasonal unemployment, which may be considerable and yet produce but modest seasonal amplitudes, if seasons differ with different industries.[3]

Other business-cycle specialists could, of course, be quoted to similar effect.[4] Changes in the level of employment can thus be said to

[3] *Business Cycles,* pp. 510-511. The footnote on page 504 reads: "There is really no such thing as a theory of total output as such, in the full sense of the word, for this would imply that we are able to represent it as an explicit and uniquely determined variable in function of some independent variables of the same, i.e., the systematic, class—such as price level, interest rate, quantity of circulating medium. Our whole analysis shows this to be impossible and any theory that attempts it, to be a sham. What we mean above is simply theoretical expectation as to behavior of output within a process that simultaneously shapes all the variables."

[4] Compare, for example, G. Haberler, *Prosperity and Depression,* 3d ed., pp. 260-261.

be our primary datum about the cycle only if the cycle is defined in a very special way, and the idea that a cycle theory ought to be based on a theory of employment has little to recommend it. This is clearly not the place to take up Keynes's own attempt at formulating a theory of the cycle in terms of his theory of employment. We limit ourselves to three remarks, the implications of which seem to us obvious, and the truth of which may be readily verified:

1. Keynes's "Notes on the Trade Cycle" in the *General Theory* is a far cry from his treatment of the same subject in the *Treatise on Money*. Professor Schumpeter's views on innovation were "unreservedly accepted" [5] in the *Treatise,* but there is no trace of them in the *General Theory.*

2. The trade cycle discussed in Keynes's "Notes" is not the Kitchin cycle, but the Juglar.[6]

3. The "Notes" are concerned with the typical cycle of the Nineteenth Century,[7] and there are no grounds for a suspicion that the conditions of Trustified Capitalism are relevant.

Innovation and the Nature of Competition

An essential element in Marxist doctrine is the idea that competitive capitalism is a phase of economic development preliminary to monopoly capitalism, and that the growth of monopoly sets the stage for the final act in the drama of capitalist evolution.[8]

---

[5] *Treatise,* pp. 95-96. Compare L. Klein, *The Keynesian Revolution,* p. 16n. Unless this note is meant to refer strictly to the *Treatise,* we cannot agree that Keynes' cycle theory has much in common with that of Professor Schumpeter. It is worth observing that there is nothing in Keynes' *Treatise* to suggest that he had ever read the *Theorie der wirtschaftlichen Entwicklung.* Whatever may be thought of Mitchell's summary *(Business Cycles: The Problem and Its Setting,* 1927, pp. 20-22), it was not intended to be a substitute for the original work, and it made no very lasting impression on Keynes.

[6] The contraction alone is supposed to average from three to five years. See *General Theory,* p. 317. Whatever is to be salvaged from the Notes must, however, be applied chiefly to the Kitchins. Compare, for example, the work of Professor Metzler on inventory cycles included in the Bibliography.

[7] See *General Theory,* p. 314. The "nineteenth-century environment" is the context for the whole subsequent discussion.

[8] See P. M. Sweezy, *Socialism,* pp. 150ff. Compare also the same author's *Theory of Capitalist Development,* especially Chapter XV.

Remarkably similar views are held by a great many economists who would hardly count themselves as Marxist communicants. The general position may briefly, and with less than extreme accuracy, be stated as follows. In former times, laissez faire could be relied upon to promote economic well-being, since enterprise was characterized by the presence of numerous, small-scale units, each of which in the pursuit of profit tended to maximize output and minimize unit costs. More recently, the scale of enterprise has greatly increased; prices have come to be adminstered by management, rather than determined in competitive markets; and the maintenance of high prices and restriction of output are responsible for many of our modern problems, notably that of unemployment.

The point of view thus sketchily suggested is the subject matter of a voluminous literature,[9] and it has played an important role in fluctuating public policies toward business enterprise. Manifestly, we cannot hope to do justice to the questions involved, but for the purposes of this study it will be sufficient to dispose of one false issue.

From the standpoint of the Schumpeterian System, an element of monopoly enters necessarily into the process of innovation. Even in an otherwise purely competitive economy, the entrepreneur who founds a firm to produce a new product must enjoy, for a time, a monopoly position. In a world of larger-scale enterprises, innovation may be practicable only if some measures are taken to protect the firm's advantage over an interval during which the reward may be collected. This aspect of the model has been developed in considerable detail, and it has been shown that most of the practices commonly associated with monopolies fall within the framework of the Schumpeterian System.

Unfortunately, this has been interpreted to mean that Professor Schumpeter has taken a stand in defense of monopoly,[10] and has developed an apology for monopoly tactics that few are eager to accept. The issue has been put as follows:

> The only question at issue, therefore, is one of fact: Are the achievements of capitalist enterprise in the past directly imputable to the

[9] An excellent exposition that has the additional merit of brevity has been written by Professor Ellis. See H. S. Ellis, "Monopoly and Employment," *Prices, Wages, and Employment,* pp. 67-94.
[10] Compare *Capitalism, Socialism, and Democracy,* Preface to the Second Edition, 1947, p. x.

presence of monopolistic protections, or rather to highly competitive conditions of entry and of sale? Schumpeter assumes the former to be the case throughout his argument, and it is this assumption which calls for careful examination.[11]

If there really were such an issue, it would be necessary to agree that not much could be said for Professor Schumpeter's position. The fact is, however, that in the Schumpeterian System it is not a matter of monopoly *versus* competition in the ordinary sense, but rather one of innovation in a process of creative destruction. In comparison with the static concept of entry, the competition due to innovation is as much more effective as is bombardment in comparison with forcing a door.[12] The turnpike, the canal, and the railroad might all be able to prevent entry in the static sense, but none could prevent the development of other forms of transportation. Steel firms feel the competition of aluminum, and the producers of both these metals are hit by the makers of plastics. Instances might be multiplied indefinitely, but the point requires no further elaboration. The impact of innovation on existing firms is the competition that really counts in the Schumpeterian System.

It should be observed that there is nothing in this that even implies that all monopoly is desirable.[13] If anyone cares to draw a conclusion applicable to public policy from the model, his inference would have to be that every existing case should be dealt with on its own merits, and that it might be well to devote more energy to keeping innovation going than to breaking up existing structures directly. That is, of course, assuming that he has in mind the preservation of the capitalist system.[14] If he prefers to save capitalism by putting it beyond the reach of mankind, he may reach another result. On all such questions the Schumpeterian System is neutral.[15]

---

[11] G. H. Hildebrand, Jr., "Monopolization and the Decline of Investment Opportunity," *American Economic Review,* September, 1943, p. 592.

[12] See *Capitalism, Socialism, and Democracy,* p. 84.

[13] Compare E. S. Mason in "The Effectiveness of the Federal Antitrust Laws: A Symposium," *American Economic Review,* June, 1949, pp. 712-713, for a recent statement in which this is clearly recognized.

[14] Compare D. M. Wright, *Democracy and Progress,* especially Chapter VIII.

[15] Though some readers find it hard to believe. Compare *Capitalism, Socialism, and Democracy,* Preface to the Second Edition.

Innovation and Investment Opportunity

Up to this point, our discussion of the impact of innovation may have made it appear that its effects are mainly destructive. The Schumpeterian System has, in fact, been said to neglect the favorable effects of innovation on investment opportunity, and to concentrate too heavily on the unfavorable ones. In a paper on the repercussions of investment, Mr. Lachmann argues that the Keynesians have stressed those repercussions due to the substitutability of capital, while ignoring those due to complementarity.[16] He then goes on to say:

> Our argument rests on the realization that all investment is a dynamic process, and relies on capital complementarity and the favorable investment repercussions it engenders as the main vehicle of change.
>
> In Professor Schumpeter's theory, on the other hand, the relationship between entrepreneurs and the "old firms," as well as among the entrepreneurs themselves, is essentially competitive and substitutive. In spite of occasional hints at possible favorable effects of complementarity, . . . it is clear that he regards competition as the main vehicle of dynamic change.[17]

It is true that the Keynesians have relied heavily on a fall in the marginal efficiency of capital as investment proceeds, both cyclically and in the long run. The suggestion that anything remotely similar can be said of the Schumpeterian System must, however, be rejected. In fact, the concept of complementarity is hardly adequate to bring out the effects of innovation on investment opportunity in this schema. One of the most impressive features of Professor Schumpeter's model is the quantitative magnitude of the investment

[16] L. M. Lachmann, "Investment Repercussions," *Quarterly Journal of Economics*, November, 1948, p. 712. Professor Hayek's paper, "Investment That Raises the Demand for Capital," was one of the first treatments of complementarity, but not the only one prior to 1948. Professor Angell's *Investment and Business Cycles* deals with the matter, as does Professor Fellner's *Monetary Policies and Full Employment*.

[17] "Investment Repercussions," p. 712n. The part of this quotation omitted from the text consists of a reference to *Business Cycles*, p. 134, which reads: "They proceed not exclusively under the stimulus of loss. For some of the 'old' firms new opportunities for expansion open up: the new methods or commodities create New Economic Space."

identified with the impact of major innovations.   Since this fact appears to be in some danger of being overlooked, let us try to drive the point home.

A number of attempts have been made to estimate the amount of investment generated by particular innovations.   Consider, for example, the following estimate of the investment in related industries occasioned by automobiles in the nineteen-twenties:

> If we add to the amount spent for motor vehicles in that decade the investment in automotive manufacturing facilities, and, say, one-half the investment in streets and roads, in petroleum extraction and refining, and in pipe lines, we arrive at a figure of about 16 per cent of all capital formation.   What the percentage would be with a *complete* coverage of investment induced in related industries we cannot say, but since we have included those most important from an investment standpoint it seems probable that it would still be well under 20.   A similar inclusion of related industries for the peak decade of the railroads would probably also yield a percentage well below this figure, and for the electrical industries it would be scarcely more than half of it.[18]

We may next refer to Professor Hansen's well-known estimate of the comparative importance of the factors responsible for nineteenth-century investment as a whole:

> These figures, while only suggestive, point unmistakably to the conclusion that the opening of new territory and the growth of population were together responsible for a very large fraction—possibly somewhere near one-half—of the total volume of new capital formation in the nineteenth century.[19]

Lifted from its context, this statement may seem to play down the role of innovation, leaving to technological development not much more than half the credit for aggregate capital formation.   Professor Hansen, however, continues:

> . . . the progress of technology itself played in the nineteenth century a decisive role in the opening of new territory and as a stimulus to population growth.[20]

---

[18] G. Terborgh, *The Bogey of Economic Maturity,* p. 87.
[19] A. H. Hansen, *Fiscal Policy and Business Cycles,* p. 160.
[20] *Fiscal Policy and Business Cycles,* p. 161.

Similarly, in his testimony before the Temporary National Economic Committee, Professor Hansen said:

> The enormous capital outlays of the nineteenth century were, of course, in the first instance conditioned by new technological developments . . .[21]

Now, from our standpoint, the important thing to observe is that these estimates, large as they are, by no means exceed what we should expect from Professor Schumpeter's model. The estimate for the automobile industry indeed falls far short of the proper order of magnitude. The automobile completely changed the conditions of life for the people of this country, and there was scarcely a firm or household that did not feel its effects. Not only were countless investment opportunities opened for suppliers, dealers, garages, repair shops, taxi services, bus lines, filling stations, tires and tubes, and so on almost without end, but a whole agricultural revolution was only a part of the picture. Steel, copper, rubber, glass, railroad transportation, automobile insurance, were directly stimulated; and a great volume of construction, both industrial and domestic, was induced.[22]

Recalling that the opening of new territory is innovation in the Schumpeterian System, we see that Professor Hansen is coming considerably closer to the relevant magnitude, without, however, overstating the case. As soon as new territory is included within the concept of innovation, and technology is given a "decisive role" in stimulating population growth, the investment opportunity attributable to factors other than innovation shrinks to negligible proportions. This, of course, is exactly Professor Schumpeter's position.[23]

In order to demonstrate the full impact of innovation on investment opportunities as developed in *Business Cycles,* it would be necessary to reproduce a substantial portion of that book. We shall quote only a few passages:

----

[21] *Savings and Investment,* p. 3504.
[22] See *Business Cycles,* pp. 774-777.
[23] Compare *Business Cycles,* p. 94.

The great investment in cotton planting in the South began in the recession of that Kondratieff: a typical example of an induced development or of what we have called expansion into new economic space created by previous innovation.[24]

If we are to form an idea as to the quantitative adequacy of innovation, we must bear in mind that all it should, according to our schema, be adequate for, is "ignition." What we see on the surface is largely the effect of what we have called the Secondary Wave, the phenomena of which can in fact be sufficiently expressed in terms of general conditions, growing commercial centers, independently given demand conditions, and so on. To that ignition we must, hence, always apply a multiplier before confronting it with statistical findings about social aggregates. Looked at in this manner, the development in the cotton trade alone would be adequate to explain a Kondratieff upswing.[25]

However, our insistence on the element of mere Growth should not be misunderstood. While very real, it was not anything like so important as the traditional view would suggest; for much of it was induced innovation or immediate effect of innovation.[26]

Railroads, iron, steel, machinery, the emergence of a modern textile industry and of the type of financial institutions mentioned above, formed the core of the innovations of that period and were obviously adequate to induce all the investment and to produce all the phenomena of that prosperity which in 1856 tapered off into what contemporaneous reports describe as overproduction. We shall have little difficulty in identifying this as the effect on total output of those innovations and their subsidiaries.[27]

The writer frankly despairs of his ability to give, within the space at his command, anything like an adequate picture, both of the ramifications of the transforming influence of electricity and of the other innovations which—independently of it or induced by it—grouped themselves around it and, together with it, set a pace to output of producers' goods that, in spite of "responsive" extension of capacities, repeatedly resulted in steel and even coal "famines" or conditions approaching serious shortage.[28]

---

[24] *Business Cycles,* p. 269.
[25] *Business Cycles,* pp. 274-275.
[26] *Business Cycles,* p. 285n.
[27] *Business Cycles,* p. 361.
[28] *Business Cycles,* p. 413.

With respect to the concept of complementarity, one final remark may be made. This term either implies, or may easily be taken to imply, that the impact of innovation may be meaningfully treated from the standpoint of relationships between the attributes of different types of capital goods. In other words, attention tends to be concentrated on the form taken by investment to the exclusion of broader and more important considerations. A railroad, for instance, may be thought of as consisting of an aggregation of rails, rolling stock, and so on, but there is nothing about the relation between this equipment and other capital goods that serves to explain the impact of innovation on the economy.[29] Not only must a railroad be built in a particular region; it must also be properly established as a business enterprise. Most important of all, it must be introduced at the right time.

In the Schumpeterian System, the impact of an innovation depends upon the phases of the cycles in which it is introduced. A "given" innovation introduced in equilibrium would yield a whole primary and secondary wave of repercussions, and could fairly be said to account for every dollar of investment that followed. The same innovation introduced just before the break in the secondary wave would merely be swallowed up in the ensuing liquidation, and would open no investment opportunities of any consequence. In Professor Schumpeter's words:

> One essential peculiarity of the working of the capitalist system is that it imposes sequences and rules of timing. Its effectiveness largely rests on this and on the promptness with which it punishes infringement of those sequences and rules. For success in capitalist society it is not sufficient to be right *in abstracto;* one must be right at given dates.[30]

There is thus a special sense in which the Schumpeterian System may be regarded as historical. The model as a whole, of course, represents the economic process of a particular historical epoch. But beyond this, what happens within the model depends not merely on functional time, but on historic time. In other words,

---

[29] Compare W. Isard, "Transport Development and Building Cycles," *Quarterly Journal of Economics,* November, 1942, especially pp. 92, 95, 98, and 101-103.

[30] *Business Cycles,* p. 412.

the Schumpeterian System is a dynamic, historical [31] model of the capitalist process.

INNOVATION AND THE NATURE OF BUSINESS CYCLES

One of the most fundamental criticisms of the Schumpeterian System is that the model is so remote from statistical fact that no links between theory and reality can be satisfactorily established. This criticism has far-reaching implications for all economic analysis, and most immediately for the nature of business cycles. Professor Kuznets has written:

> One cannot well escape the impression that Professor Schumpeter's model in its present state cannot be linked directly and clearly with statistically observed realities; that the extreme paucity of statistical analysis in the treatise in an inevitable result of the type of theoretical model adopted; and that the great reliance upon historical outlines and qualitative discussion is a consequence of the difficulty of devising statistical procedures that would correspond to the theoretical model . . .
>
> The cycle is essentially a quantitative concept. All its characteristics such as duration, amplitude, phases, etc., can be conceived only as measurable aspects, and can be properly measured only with the help of quantitative data.
>
> To establish the existence of cycles of a given type requires first a demonstration that fluctuations of that approximate duration recur, with fair simultaneity, in the movements of various significant aspects of economic life (production and employment in various industries, prices of various groups of goods, interest rates, volumes of trade, flow of credit, etc.); and second, an indication of what external factors or peculiarities of the economic system proper account for such recurrent fluctuations.[32]

It is evident that the first passage represents a valid criticism of the Schumpeterian System only if the statements that follow it are accepted without question. Is it true, however, that the cycle is necessarily a quantitative concept? This is the heart of the problem, for

---

[31] We are using Professor Samuelson's terminology. See P. A. Samuelson, "Dynamics, Statics, and the Stationary State," *Review of Economic Statistics,* February, 1943, pp. 58-61. Compare the same author's *Foundations of Economic Analysis,* pp. 311-317.

[32] S. S. Kuznets, "Schumpeter's Business Cycles," *American Economic Review,* June, 1940, pp. 266-267. We have omitted some matter not relevant to the present argument.

unless this statement is correct, the rest of the criticism may be disregarded.

Anyone is naturally free to define the cycle in any way he pleases, but we may take it for granted that the identification of cycles with quantitative phenomena is intended to be more than a mere matter of taste in this context. Let us see what some of the leading students of business cycles have to say on the question.

Professors Burns and Mitchell define business cycles as follows:

> Business cycles are a type of fluctuation found in the aggregate economic activity of nations that organize their work mainly in business enterprises: a cycle consists of expansions occurring at about the same time in many economic activities, followed by similarly general recessions, contractions, and revivals which merge into the expansion phase of the next cycle; this sequence of changes is recurrent but not periodic; in duration business cycles vary from more than one year to ten or twelve years; they are not divisible into shorter cycles of similar character with amplitudes approximating their own.[33]

With Professor Hawtrey:

> The trade cycle is composed of periods of good trade, characterized by rising prices and low unemployment percentages, alternating with periods of bad trade, characterized by falling prices and high unemployment percentages.[34]

With Professor Haberler:

> We may conclude that a combination of the three indices—(1) employment, (2) real income consumed and (3) real income produced—can be regarded as the criterion of the existence, and measure of the degree, of prosperity and depression and changes in the same. If all three indices point in the same direction, the situation is clear. If they diverge, it is as a rule possible to arrive at some indication on the basis of the considerations set forth.[35]

---

[33] A. F. Burns and W. C. Mitchell, *Measuring Business Cycles*, p. 3. The authors discuss some of the problems raised by their definition in the pages immediately following.

[34] R. G. Hawtrey, "The Trade Cycle," *Readings in Business Cycle Theory*, pp. 330-349; quotation from p. 331. The article originally appeared in the Dutch publication *De Economist* in 1925, and was reprinted as Chapter 5 in Professor Hawtrey's *Trade and Credit*, 1928.

[35] G. Haberler, *Prosperity and Depression*, 3d ed., p. 263.

Finally, with Professor Hansen:

> The fluctuations of cyclical movements may be characterized in terms of either money income, real income (the output of material goods and services), or employment. These three categories, to be sure, are not identical. Money income is a function both of real income and of price movements, while real income or output differs from employment by reason of changes in productivity. Cyclically, however, the three move more or less in consonance, though the trend movement is likely to differ considerably under varying circumstances. For certain problems it is extremely important to differentiate sharply between them. But frequently in discussing economic fluctuations or cyclical movements all three may be regarded without serious error as moving together, whether in the upswing or in the downswing. This is particularly true for the short-run movements but less true for the longer-run developments.[36]

In the same discussion, Professor Hansen adds:

> The most general, all-inclusive statement of the essential character of cyclical movements is that they consist in the increase or decline, as the case may be, in the purchase of real investment goods and of durable consumers' goods as defined above.[37]

These careful statements have both similarities and differences, but the important characteristic they possess in common is, from our standpoint, the emphasis on measurable aggregates. Cycles are identified with the behavior of particular time series, and the definitions are formulated in terms of these series. Professors Burns and Mitchell are least specific as to what series they have in mind, but nobody familiar with their work can doubt that by the term "activities" they mean phenomena subject to statistical measurement.

Now let us compare Professor Schumpeter's definition of cycles with those reproduced above. The "formal definition" given in *Business Cycles* is as follows:

> By the term *cycle* we designate the fact, that a given series corrected for seasonal displays recurrence of values either in its items or in its first or higher time derivatives more than once.[38]

---

[36] A. H. Hansen, *Fiscal Policy and Business Cycles*, pp. 14-15.
[37] *Fiscal Policy and Business Cycles*, p. 16.
[38] *Business Cycles*, p. 200.

This definition, however, occurs in a discussion of statistical method, in which the object is merely to distinguish between cycles and trends in an individual time series. The statement therefore sheds little light on what business cycles in general are supposed to be. It would seem that we are entitled to something more definite in a two-volume treatise on the subject, but if so we are doomed to disappointment. If any clear and concise statement as to exactly what business cycles are is contained in the book, it is remarkably well concealed. Instead of starting with a neat definition, or even of developing one in the course of the analysis, the question seems to be continually avoided, and what we find are such statements as the following:

> . . . it is absurd to think that we can derive the contour lines of our phenomena from our statistical material only. All we could ever prove from it is that no regular contour lines exist.[39]

> We cannot stress this point sufficiently. General history (social, political, and cultural), economic history, and more particularly industrial history are not only indispensable but really the most important contributors to the understanding of our problem. All other materials and methods, statistical and theoretical, are only subservient to them and worse than useless without them.[40]

> The time sequences we observe are, of course, part of our material from which we have to start and for which we have to account. And we have to bring every new factual finding into accord with the rest of the facts of the economic process and not with any poetry of ours. But no statistical finding can ever either prove or disprove a proposition which we have reason to believe by virtue of simpler and more fundamental facts.[41]

> We must not trust our graphs implicitly. Both peaks and troughs may easily mislead and it is hardly an exaggeration to say that, as far as information about fundamental processes goes, they are precisely the most unreliable items in an array.[42]

To a student trained to think in quantitative terms this sort of thing is hardly satisfactory. He is bound to feel that everything

---

[39] *Business Cycles,* p. 13.
[40] *Business Cycles,* p. 13.
[41] *Business Cycles,* p. 33.
[42] *Business Cycles,* pp. 150-151.

clear and precise is being pushed to one side, and that a vague and nebulous cyclical pattern is being shored up by a dubious use of the materials. What, he wants to know, are these cycles anyway? How can four phases be assigned to a cycle that cannot even be plotted on a chart? Is Professor Schumpeter really following a path through his vast array of facts, or is he using the facts in such a way as to create the illusion that such a path exists when it is not there at all? To these questions there can be only one answer. If innovation and qualitative change are the fundamental elements in economic development, then no amount of quantitative analysis can reveal the really significant pattern. As soon as we open the door to qualitative phenomena, we admit a degree of human judgment that must largely supplant more objective and mechanical devices. There is no neat definition of business cycles in Professor Schumpeter's treatise simply because it would be impossible to give one. The whole Schumpeterian System must be mastered in order to understand what business cycles are:

> Analyzing business cycles means neither more nor less than analyzing the economic process of the capitalist era. Most of us discover this truth which at once reveals the nature of the task and also its formidable dimensions. Cycles are not, like tonsils, separable things that might be treated by themselves, but are, like the beat of the heart, of the essence of the organism that displays them. I have called this book "Business Cycles" in order to indicate succinctly what the reader is to expect, but the subtitle really renders what I have tried to do.[43]

Business cycles, then, are identical with the capitalist process of which the driving force is innovation. Does anyone wish to deny this? Apparently not. "The essential feature of history is the emergence of novelty." [44] But if we admit the truth of this, what becomes of the notion that the cycle is essentially a quantitative concept? We cannot have it both ways at once, and unless innovation is completely excluded from consideration, the cycle becomes qualitative as well as quantitative, and our confidence in the virtues of statistical time series is diminished accordingly.

Let us have no misunderstanding. There is more than one

---

[43] *Business Cycles,* opening paragraph of the Preface.
[44] A. P. Usher, "The Significance of Modern Empiricism for History and Economics," *Journal of Economic History,* November, 1949, p. 149.

method of studying business cycles, and it is well that there should be some specialization.   The specialist makes his contribution, however, within limits of his own choosing, and no amount of concentrated quantitative analysis can get out of the data more than they contain.   Working definitions that serve the purposes of some particular approach may well be inadequate for synthesis on a larger scale.[45]   Unless some serious flaw can be found in the Schumpeterian System, the fact that it cannot be neatly fitted into statistical data does not constitute a valid objection to the model.

[45] See S. S. Kuznets, "Statistics and Economic History," *Journal of Economic History*, May, 1941, pp. 26-41, for a good discussion of the need for combining historical and theoretical-statistical research.   See also the same author's review of Professor Hansen's *Fiscal Policy and Business Cycles*, *Review of Economic Statistics*, February, 1942, pp. 31-36, where the importance of technological change is particularly stressed.

Chapter 9

THE THREE-CYCLE SCHEMA

We come now to a group of problems raised by Professor Schumpeter's three-cycle schema. In this chapter a number of general issues arising out of his presentation will be treated, while reserving for the following chapter the more spectacular issues associated with the phenomenon of the long wave.

The three-cycle schema is the practical or working result of the refusal to accept a single-cycle hypothesis. Once that hypothesis was rejected, the three-cycle presentation was settled upon as leading to maximum returns. However, in the historical exposition of cycles in the nineteenth century little use could be made of the Kitchin cycle because of the relative paucity of data for that period.

Before we deal with the difficulties that some people have associated with the three-cycle presentation, it is well to place in its proper perspective Professor Schumpeter's role in the development of that schema. The particular cycles involved, of course, are not discoveries of Professor Schumpeter; indeed, credit is liberally bestowed upon others.[1] Nor is their combination into an interrelated whole an innovation by Professor Schumpeter, who calls attention to a somewhat similar schema advanced earlier by Kitchin.[2] This is not to deny that the emphasis upon a three-cycle schema, as well as the underlying unity of explanation, is a novelty with Professor Schumpeter. Finally, it is worth observing that the adoption of the schema was not new with him in *Business Cycles*, but had been advanced by him on several previous occasions.[3] Indeed, if we may judge by the

---

[1] *Business Cycles,* pp. 164-165.
[2] J. Kitchin, "Cycles and Trends in Economic Factors," *Review of Economic Statistics,* January, 1923, pp. 10-16. As Mr. G. Garvy points out, Kondratieff advanced a three-cycle model in 1926. "Kondratieff's Theory of Long Cycles," *Review of Economic Statistics,* November, 1943, p. 207.
[3] See "The Present World Depression: A Tentative Diagnosis," *American Economic Review,* March, 1931, pp. 179-182; also p. ix, Preface to the English Edition, *The Theory of Economic Development,* 1934; and "The Analysis of Economic Change," *Review of Economic Statistics,* May, 1935, pp. 2-10.

published comments of critics—which is perhaps not permissible in this case—the schema was accepted in 1930 at the annual meeting of the American Economic Association.[4]

Upon a number of occasions the validity of one or more of the particular cycles involved in the three-cycle schema has been denied; none more frequently than that of the long wave. However, the three reasons for expecting various types of cycles have not been challenged in the critical literature. We cannot emphasize too strongly that a rejection of one or more cycles of the three-cycle schema—should this turn out to be necessary—would not permit us to return to the single-cycle hypothesis, unless the reasons for expecting multiplicity can be successfully challenged.

The issues that have been raised in the critical literature having to do with the three-cycle schema are dealt with in this chapter under the following headings:

1. Statistical difficulties are associated with identifying different orders of equilibrium. Each type of cycle is supposed to arise out of a neighborhood of equilibrium. How can one, let alone three, equilibrium neighborhoods be identified, statistically or otherwise?

2. The three-cycle schema yields a rigid picture of reality. Each higher-order cycle contains an integral number of lower-order cycles, so that reality is apparently poured into an inflexible mold.

3. The theory of the three cycles is a mechanical but loose application of the theory of the Juglar to the other cycles.

4. A transport-building cycle should be added to the three cycles already identified.

Identification of Different Orders of Equilibrium

In the Schumpeterian System different types of innovation give rise to different types of business cycles. These cycles are related, in that the sweep of each longer wave provides neighborhoods of equilibrium for the wave of the next lower order. Thus, corresponding to each cycle is a particular order of equilibrium.

What is the logical meaning of these various orders of equilibrium? Kondratieff attempted to identify the different orders with the Mar-

---

[4] The critics who addressed themselves to Professor Schumpeter's remarks were Professor Hansen and Willard L. Thorp. See footnotes 7 and 8, Chapter 10.

shallian concepts of market, short-run and long-run equilibria.[5] It may be readily seen, however, that this cannot be done. The Schumpeterian concepts involve general rather than partial equilibrium. Moreover, the Marshallian time periods cannot be given a generalized historical connotation appropriate to all types of innovation. Instead, the higher orders of equilibrium are differing degrees of provisional equilibrium, suitable for the introduction of some but not all types of innovation. These different orders of equilibrium offer no logical difficulty but, since Professor Schumpeter wishes to associate definite historical periods of time with them, there are some who feel that the statistical difficulties are exceptionally grave.

Professor Kuznets' objections on this score are worthy of rather full quotation:

> We may pass . . . to a consideration of the four-phase model of a cycle conceived in terms of departures from an equilibrium line, and the bearing of this model upon statistical analysis of time series. The procedure preferred by Professor Schumpeter involves establishing points of inflection, first in the original series, then in the line that passes through the first series of inflection points and so on, successively decomposing the total series into several cyclical lines. Professor Schumpeter himself recognizes the difficulties involved in the application of this procedure (see page 211, vol. I). There is first the delicate problem of smoothing the series so as to eliminate the effect of erratic fluctuations on the second order differences used to establish inflection points. A more serious difficulty arises because the assumption that the inflection points are in the neighborhood of equilibrium levels implies a specific pattern of cyclical movements; and there is no ground for expecting cyclical fluctuations in actual series to conform to this pattern.
>
> For these reasons Professor Schumpeter does not recommend the method for general application and recognizes it only as a first approximation and a far from infallible guide.
>
> The difficulties encountered in the matter of inflection points and the paucity of formal statistical analysis in the treatise lead to a doubt whether Professor Schumpeter's concept of equilibrium and of the four-phase model of business cycles are such as to permit of application to statistical analysis.[6]

---

[5] G. Garvy, "Kondratieff's Theory of Long Cycles," *Review of Economic Statistics*, November, 1943, p. 207.

[6] S. Kuznets, "Schumpeter's Business Cycles," *American Economic Review*, June, 1940, pp. 264-265.

The use of inflection points, however, is not Professor Schumpeter's chief reliance in the determination of equilibrium neighborhoods; rather that reliance is upon historical analysis of a given situation. As he has himself put it:

> . . . we will emphasize . . . that historical information about each individual case is the only means by which to reduce to bearable proportions the influence of external factors and that study and discussion of each situation which seems to have some claim to being called a neighborhood of equilibrium, and unavoidably rough estimates will be the surest way to reliable results, at least for some time to come. It is this method on which the writer has chiefly relied and it is in order to illustrate principles rather than for the sake of the use we make in our work on time series (some experiments, of course, have been made) that we now attack the question of the purely statistical procedure.[7]

The practical result of the identification of different orders of equilibrium is the dating of each type of cycle from equilibrium to equilibrium. The Schumpeterian analysis provides the theoretical rationale for this. The method possesses the added advantage that the main alternative, dating from peaks or troughs, is not more satisfactory but less so. Peaks and troughs are highly subject to the influence of external factors and are perhaps the most unreliable of all items in a time series.

RIGIDITY OF THE SYSTEM

The view that lower-order cycles move about positions of equilibrium provided by higher-order cycles requires that there be an integral number of lower-order cycles in each higher-order cycle. This seems to be the main element involved in the charge of rigidity against the Schumpeterian System.[8] The necessity for this situation may be briefly explained. A cycle of intermediate duration cannot reach an equilibrium neighborhood unless the cycles of lower order playing around it have reached equilibrium. This will yield an integral number of cycles of the lower order. Furthermore, the cycle

---

[7] *Business Cycles,* p. 207.
[8] Professor Kuznets speaks of ". . . the rather rigid relationship claimed to have been established among the three groups of cycles . . . ," "Schumpeter's Business Cycles," p. 270.

of highest order cannot reach an equilibrium neighborhood for it until the intermediate cycle has reached its equilibrium neighborhood. The result, of course, may appear rigid, but it is necessary so long as we adhere to the position that each of the cycles is caused by the introduction of innovations in the various equilibrium neighborhoods.

JUGLAR THEORY MECHANICALLY EXTENDED TO OTHER CYCLES?

Another contention, somewhat similar to the above-mentioned one of rigidity, is that of Professor Lange, who

> . . . is under the impression that Professor Schumpeter has extended his theory of business cycles, worked out originally with reference to Juglars, rather mechanically to Kondratiefs and Kitchins. Such extension requires much more careful empirical and also theoretical analysis. Thus, for instance, it is doubtful whether a Kondratief cycle, even if Professor Schumpeter's theory were totally accepted, would lead to a Secondary Wave of the same type as a Juglar; the same holds for Kitchins.[9]

With respect to the part of this argument relating to the Kitchins, Professor Schumpeter has already entered a disclaimer. As he has said, ". . . it is even necessary to leave open the possibility that Kitchins are merely fluctuations of the adaptive type." [10] However, such waves of adaptation may often rely on innovation for their propelling factor.[11]

With regard to the remainder of the argument, however, there is room for doubt as to whether a mechanical extension of Juglar

---

[9] O. Lange, Review of Schumpeter's *Business Cycles, Review of Economic Statistics,* November, 1941, p. 192.

[10] *Business Cycles,* p. 171. In connection with the theory of inventory cycles Professor Schumpeter has publicly commended the work of Professor Metzler. ("The Decade of the Twenties," *American Economic Review,* May, 1946, p. 3n.) See L. Metzler, "The Nature and Stability of Inventory Cycles," *Review of Economic Statistics,* 1941, pp. 113-129; and "Business Cycles and the Modern Theory of Employment," *American Economic Review,* June, 1946, pp. 278-291. A version of the latter paper was reprinted in *The New Economics,* S. Harris, Ed., Chapter 33.

[11] Compare L. Metzler, "Business Cycles and the Modern Theory of Employment," pp. 290-291.

theory to the Kondratieff has taken place or whether Professor
Schumpeter did not take the trouble to set down the full details of
the theory for the latter cycle.[12] He perhaps did not suppose, for
example, that anyone would seriously apply the concept of abnormal liquidation to a Kondratieff cycle separately from the other
cycles. Yet this apparently has been done by one writer, with results understandably disappointing to him.[13] However, the matter
of writing down details should not be unduly stressed; a certain
amount of looseness is an inevitable result of Professor Schumpeter's
concept of the cycle. In view of the extended discussion of this subject in the previous chapter, we shall be content here with the following brief remark of Professor Schumpeter's: ". . . cycles are an
irregular phenomenon playing in an environment disturbed by additional irregularities . . ."[14]

A Transport-Building Cycle?

To some observers, the reasons for multiple cycles may be so
impressive as to cause wonder why more cycles are not identified.
Indeed, to a certain extent this is done. "Special cycles" caused by
fortuitous variations of crops are admitted.[15] Oscillations and re-

---

[12] Compare E. Rothbarth, *Economic Journal,* June-September, 1942, p. 223.
[13] See R. Fels, "The Long-Wave Depression, 1873-97," *Review of Economics
and Statistics,* February, 1949, pp. 69-73. Professor Fels says, "Professor
Schumpeter's explanation [of the last quarter of the nineteenth century]
does not appear sound insofar as it is based on the concept of abnormal
liquidation (depression phase) in a Kondratieff cycle. Abnormal liquidation has a clear meaning in the Juglar cycle. Prosperity and recession
phases of the Kondratieff likewise have a clear meaning. But it is not
easy to see why the liquidation of positions made untenable by the long
sweep of innovations—say, the decline of a city not on a main railroad line
—should degenerate into a process of liquidating positions that would be
tenable in an equilibrium position." (p. 72, brackets ours.) Professor
Fels then cites approvingly the Lange remark about "mechanical extension." However, the business situation at any given time is the resultant
of the effects of the three cycles, so that the abnormal liquidation of the
Kondratieff works through that of a Juglar. As Professor Schumpeter has
put it, ". . . the distinction between simultaneous cycles mainly turns on
the neighborhoods and . . . in the intervals between them there is not the
same kind of 'realism' about it . . .", *Business Cycles,* p. 216.
[14] *Business Cycles,* p. 174n.
[15] *Business Cycles,* pp. 178-179.

placement waves are also admitted, with appropriate qualifications.

However, it is in the case of the building cycle that probably most people who work with more than one cycle would prefer to add another cycle to the three-cycle schema. Professor Hansen explicitly does this, while Silberling and Professor Isard go so far as to speak of a separate "transport-building" cycle.[16] We shall deal first with the question of the building cycle.

Building cycles are not treated as separate cycles because ordinarily they are secondary-wave phenomena related to underlying innovations. "We have seen in the instance of building that what strongly looks like a very special movement can yet be brought within the schema of cyclical events and understood as a consequence of conditions which, in turn, can be traced to our process." [17]

As an illustration of how building cycles and other cycles, in this case the long wave, are related, Professor Schumpeter has written the following:

> Taking, for brevity's sake, dwelling-house building only, we need but list the factors that would produce supernormal activity, in order to see that the general conditions prevailing in Kondratieff downgrades and revivals—more precisely, in the prosperity phases of the shorter cycles which run their course within Kondratieff downgrades and revivals—are more favorable to the occurrence of building booms than are the general conditions prevailing in prosperities. Falling rate of interest is one of them. High rate of increase in real incomes is another: from rising or constant money incomes of the middle and lower classes, accompanied by falling cost of living, new demand for better housing will naturally follow. Innovation in the building industry or its subsidiaries will work in the same direction because, like other innovations, it is likely to spread in recession. The rise in rents that occurs during Kondratieff prosperities supplies, barring a subsequent fall in money income—which . . . is not likely to occur—an additional stimulus. Finally, industrial evolution in general means industrial migration and, moreover, migration from the countryside to the cities, both of which create new demand for construction that is eventually provided for during recession.[18]

Thus the building cycle may be readily incorporated in the Schumpeterian schema. However, for certain purposes, economists

---

[16] See N. Silberling, *The Dynamics of Business,* Chapter 10, and W. Isard, "A Neglected Cycle: The Transport-Building Cycle," *Review of Economic Statistics,* November, 1942, pp. 149-158.

[17] *Business Cycles,* p. 179.

[18] *Business Cycles,* p. 744.

may still find it convenient to work with a separate building cycle, and to this there appears no substantial objection. Can the same be said for the "transport-building" cycle, which Professor Isard argues should be added to the Schumpeterian three-cycle schema? [19]

As an empirical fact, the long waves have, in each instance, been associated with transportation improvements: canals, turnpikes, railroads, automobiles, etc. The second long wave, indeed, was dominated by railroad construction. Professor Isard, disagreeing with Professors Schumpeter and Hansen, would move these transportation innovations from the various Kondratieffs to his own cycle. Is this procedure permissible? The answer to this question must be in the negative. Many important results of transport changes are unrelated to building activity. To speak of a transport-building cycle is to run the danger of losing sight of the general cost-reducing effects of transport innovations in inducing long-wave price declines in nearly every segment of the economy.

One cannot give a place in his analytical schema both to long waves, with transport changes among the leading causal innovations, and to transport-building cycles. Professor Schumpeter has chosen to have the former, but to some, who do not believe in the existence of long waves, the latter might be preferable. We must, therefore, turn to the problems associated with the long waves.

Before that is done, however, let us notice the solution advanced by Silberling. At about the same time as Professor Isard, Silberling discovered the transport-building cycle. Furthermore, he recognized the existence of long waves. In his view, however, the long waves are caused by wars, major innovations, and political changes.[20] This solution has the merit of not leaving the long waves without causation, but we are not ready yet either to accept or to reject it. Thus, one of the issues considered in the chapter on long waves must be the relationship of those movements to external factors.

---

[19] "A Neglected Cycle: The Transport-Building Cycle," p. 156.
[20] *The Dynamics of Business,* Chapter 4, especially pp. 57-58.

Chapter 10

THE LONG WAVES

- One of the most striking features of *Business Cycles* is undoubtedly the prominent role assigned to the long waves or "Kondratieffs." To some, the elaboration given this concept may seem to be the crowning achievement of the combination of theoretical, historical, and statistical analysis. To others, however, the long waves are visible in relatively few time series, and in these unclearly and with little significance for general economic activity. Unquestionably, the long waves are among the most controversial aspects of Professor Schumpeter's work. Possibly, they are among the least understood.

Before turning to specific criticisms, let us pause to observe that the idea of a long cycle is no novelty; it has had for some time a certain measure of acceptance. Mitchell [1] gave, in 1927, a brief account of the development of the theory, and credited a Dutch economist, J. van Gelderen, with having called attention to "large cycles" in economic development as early as 1913. Van Gelderen's results were confirmed statistically by a compatriot, S. de Wolff, in 1924. Thus, cycles of some sixty years' duration were to some extent established quite independently of the work of Kondratieff. According to Mitchell's statement, Kondratieff undertook his own more extended investigations in 1922, and published his results in Russian in 1925. These results were summarized in the better-known German paper of 1926, from which Professor Stolper's familiar translation [2] was made.

Spiethoff's [3] name may be added to those mentioned by Mitchell, as having been at least a discoverer of epochs in which prosperities appeared to dominate, and of other epochs in which depressions seemed to stand out. Spiethoff did not, however, combine these epochs into cycles.

---

[1] W. C. Mitchell, *Business Cycles,* pp. 227-229.
[2] N. D. Kondratieff, "The Long Waves in Economic Life," *Review of Economic Statistics,* November, 1935, pp. 105-115.
[3] See Professor Schumpeter's remarks in *Business Cycles,* p. 164.

In the late twenties and early thirties, a number of writers seem
to have accepted these findings in varying degrees as evidence of long
waves.   Among these we may note Mitchell [4] himself, Ernest Wagemann,[5] Professors Schumpeter[6] and Hansen,[7] and possibly Willard
L. Thorp.[8]   Professors Silberling[9] and Dunlop[10] have more recently
given their support to the concept, and Professor Hansen has continued to make use of it in his own work.

In his *Fiscal Policy and Business Cycles,* Professor Hansen records
as a fact the existence of "prolonged periods of relatively good times"
and "prolonged periods of more or less chronic depression, within

---

[4] Mitchell considered the long waves to be empirically established, but was
not satisfied that they had been explained.   See Mitchell's *Business Cycles,*
p. 229.

[5] E. Wagemann, *Economic Rhythm,* Chapter V.   Wagemann accepted the
long waves for German money volume series (p. 78).   His tentative explanation stressed wars, gold, and, for the depressed 1870's and 1880's,
colonization (pp. 82-83).   The German edition of his book, *Konjunktur-
lehre,* was published in 1928.

[6] J. A. Schumpeter, "The Present World Depression: A Tentative Diagnosis," *American Economic Review, Supplement,* March, 1931, pp. 179-183.
The paper was read at the annual meeting of the American Economic
Association, December, 1930.   "So far the existence of three kinds of waves
(the 'long waves,' then what may be termed the Juglar cycle, and finally
the forty-month cycle) seem to be established with greater or less certainty."
(p. 179)

[7] A. H. Hansen, "The Business Depression of Nineteen Hundred Thirty—
Discussion," *American Economic Review,* Supplement, March, 1931, pp.
198-201.   "To understand the severity of the present crisis it is necessary,
I think, to stress the significance of the long waves to which Professor
Schumpeter alluded."   (p. 199)   See also Professor Hansen's *Economic
Stabilization in an Unbalanced World,* 1932, p. 95.

[8] W. L. Thorp, "The Business Depression of Nineteen Hundred Thirty—
Discussion," pp. 196-198.   On p. 197 Professor Schumpeter's diagnosis in
terms of his three-cycle schema is summarized without unfavorable comment.

[9] N. J. Siberling, *The Dynamics of Business,* Chapter 4.

[10] J. T. Dunlop, "The Development of Labor Organization: A Theoretical
Framework," *Insights into Labor Issues,* especially pp. 191-192.   Other
names might have been added to the list, which is not meant to be complete.   Reference should perhaps be made to C. Clark, *The Economics of
1960,* Chapter VII, especially pp. 88-96, and attention called to the remark
about Professor Robertson, p. 89n., for whatever it may be worth.   Compare also T. Wilson, *Fluctuations in Income and Employment,* index references to Kondratieff cycle.

which, however, the swings of the business cycle occur." [11] More-over, as may be seen from the following quotation, Professor Hansen substantially agrees with the Schumpeterian explanation of these periods:

> Thus, on balance, we conclude that gold and monetary factors play a subsidiary role and that the main causes of the long periods of good times and of chronic depression must be sought in technological and innovational factors, and at times in greater or less degree in the fiscal policies of governments hitherto related mainly to the conduct of war. [12]

Despite the fact that the concept of the long waves is not without adherents, it must be recognized that the idea has, in recent years, been under heavy attack. Indeed, its current status may be said to be well on the down grade. Specific criticisms, some of which have been made by partial adherents, fall into three categories:

1. First, there is the question of statistical evidence. What particular time series are supposed to reveal the long waves? Are they to be found in physical production series, or only in value series? If only in the latter, then how can they be significant?

2. Second, there is the problem of causation. If long waves can be found, can they not be accounted for by wars, political changes, and influences stemming from gold? To the extent that the waves are limited statistically to value series, the Schumpeterian explanation is felt to be unacceptable, and external factors assume a primary role.

3. Finally, it is objected that the Kondratieffs, if they exist at all, are not true cycles. If eras or epochs of good and bad times have occurred in the past, the feeling is that we ought to let it go at that, and not refer to such phenomena as cycles.

WHERE ARE THE LONG WAVES TO BE FOUND?

The outstanding names in the American literature in connection with this criticism are those of Professor Kuznets, Mr. George Garvy, and Professors Arthur F. Burns and Wesley C. Mitchell. Speaking of "the establishment of the Kondratieff cycles," Professor Kuznets says:

---

[11] Pp. 27-28.
[12] *Fiscal Policy and Business Cycles*, p. 38.

To establish the existence of cycles of a given type requires first a demonstration that fluctuations of that approximate duration recur, with fair simultaneity, in the movements of various significant aspects of economic life (production and employment in various industries, prices of various groups of goods, interest rates, volumes of trade, flow of credit, etc.); and second, an indication of what external factors or peculiarities of the economic system proper account for such recurrent fluctuations. Unless the former basis is laid, the cycle type distinguished cannot be accepted as affecting economic life at large—it may be specific to a limited part of the country's economic system. Unless the second, theoretical, basis is established there is no link that connects findings relating to empirical observations of a given type of cycles in a given country over a given period of time with the broader realm of already established knowledge.

Neither of these bases has ever been satisfactorily laid for the Kondratieff cycles. Kondratieff's own statistical analysis refers largely to price indexes, interest rates, or volumes of activity in current prices—series necessarily dominated by the price peaks of the Napoleonic wars, of the 1870's (not unconnected with the Civil War in this country), and of the World War. The prevalence of such fifty-year cycles in volumes of production, either total or for important branches of activity, in employment, in physical volume of trade, has not been demonstrated; nor has the presumed existence of these cycles been reconciled with those of a duration from 18 to 25 years established for a number of production series in this and other countries. Nor has a satisfactory theory been advanced as to why these 50-year swings should recur: the explanations tend to emphasize external factors (inventions, wars, etc.) without demonstrating their cyclical character in their tendency to recur as a result of an underlying mechanism or as effects of another group of external factors of proven "cyclicity." [13]

Thus, Professor Kuznets has serious doubts concerning "the particular aspect of activity that is considered as revealing the Kondratieff cycles," as well as doubts about the causation of these alleged cycles—the second issue to be discussed here. Before dealing with the first question raised by Professor Kuznets,[14] let us notice the objection made by Mr. Garvy, which is of a similar nature.

Mr. Garvy has published a most valuable survey of the Russian literature pertaining to the work of Kondratieff.[15] In the course of

[13] "Schumpeter's Business Cycles," *American Economic Review*, June, 1940, p. 267.
[14] Compare also W. W. Rostow, *British Economy of the Nineteenth Century*, p. 29. See note 19, Chapter 6 in this book.
[15] G. Garvy, "Kondratieff's Theory of Long Cycles," *Review of Economic Statistics*, November, 1943, pp. 203-220.

a detailed criticism of Kondratieff's statistical findings, Mr. Garvy shows "that the existence of long swings could not be proved in the production series studied by Kondratieff . . ." He then concludes:

> Although the hypothesis of cyclical swings of long duration, upon which shorter cyclical movements are superimposed, should be discarded, the view that the capitalist economy has passed through several successive stages of development characterized by different rates of growth and geographical expansion deserves attention.[16]

Professor Kuznets and Mr. Garvy share with Kondratieff himself the expectation that long waves will be found, if at all, in most of the principal time series of economic life. Nor is this expectation confined to them alone. Numerous writers appear to accept the existence of long waves in price data, and in data strongly influenced by prices. Upon failing to find similar evidence in data of other types, they tend to dismiss the long waves as lacking in general economic significance. This, however, does not follow.

Consider, for instance, an index of the general price level, or of some of its major components. Such an index may be viewed with tolerable accuracy as the product of the interaction between aggregate demand and aggregate supply. Or, if we prefer, we may limit ourselves to a statistical truism, and identify the price level as the ratio of the monetary national income to the real national income. If long waves show in price indices, they therefore reflect shifts in the ratio between two basic economic aggregates, and are hence suggestive of changes in the main sectors of economic activity.

When we further observe that the upsurges of prices characteristic of the early phases of the long cycles are associated with innovating activity productive of revolutionary changes in the economy, we no longer find it necessary to assume that the price level and the physical volume of production will invariably move together in the same direction. Moreover, the emphasis on innovation is inconsistent with the expectation that long waves should stand out clearly in individual output series.

Thus, the Schumpeterian version of the Kondratieffs does not call for the same type of statistical support that was sought by Kondratieff himself. On the contrary, if much such evidence were forthcoming, it would tell against, rather than for, the Schumpeterian

---

[16] P. 219.

System.   In a world in which innovation is at the center of cyclical movements, the establishment of long waves in price and value series is quite sufficient.[17]

Professors Burns and Mitchell are highly skeptical of the long waves even in wholesale prices.   They observe that the short-term trend of prices does not always agree with the long-term trend characteristic of a particular phase of an alleged long wave.[18]   This observation, it seems to us, counts in favor of a multicycle approach, rather than against the long wave.   They also contend that ". . . back of the 1870's the long waves are partly an optical illusion." [19] After discussing difficulties for Germany and France, they argue:

> In the United States the long waves in wholesale prices are also to some extent illusory.   High rather than rising prices prevailed from 1797 to 1812.   Again, if we concentrate on the period from about 1825 to 1860 and disregard the preceding and following years, we might describe prices as moving along a horizontal trend.   The long waves are clearest in Great Britain; yet one who did not already know these waves in advance might conclude that the trend of prices was not falling from 1823 to 1841, or rising during 1853-71.[20]

These difficulties arise from the study of a single time series in isolation, and disappear when proper account is taken of the economic history of the period.

Professors Burns and Mitchell also raise another related problem: "Whether there is evidence that the business cycles occurring during the upswings of the long waves in commodity prices differ substan-

---

[17] It is worth recalling that Commons found the long waves in prices to be of historical importance in labor history, and that others have found them to have historical significance of a broad character.   Note also the following from N. S. B. Gras and H. M. Larson, *Casebook in American Business History*, p. 662: "The hypothesis on which these cases are based is that there have been secular trends in business profits and in the ease or difficulty of business management, which correspond roughly to secular trends in prices.   The hypothesis had its origin in general observations and in the study of the experience of many firms."   Professor Gras emphasizes the importance of these trends in his *Business and Capitalism*.

[18] A. F. Burns and W. C. Mitchell, *Measuring Business Cycles*, p. 438.

[19] *Measuring Business Cycles*, p. 440.   "Better" results for the 1840's in the United States may be obtained from the index in W. B. Smith and A. H. Cole, *Fluctuations in American Business*, 1790-1860.

[20] *Measuring Business Cycles*, p. 440.

tially from the business cycles during the downswings in prices." [21]
Seven specific cycles are used in an effort to answer this question, the
cycles being deflated clearings, pig iron production, railroad stock
prices, shares traded, call money rates, railroad bond yields, and
freight car orders.

The conclusions reached by these authors were as follows:

> The thing that stands out above everything else is that the relations
> among the cyclical patterns of the activities represented in our sample
> are broadly similar during the periods of upswing and downswing in
> commodity prices. If we drop the extreme cycle of 1927-33, the refer-
> ence-cycle patterns of at least three series—deflated clearings, pig iron
> production, and railroad stock prices—are nearly indistinguishable dur-
> ing periods of upswing and downswing in prices. The only series in
> which the direction of the "trend" of prices clearly makes a substantial
> difference is railroad bond yields. That result is not surprising, since it
> has often been alleged that long-term interest rates are characterized by
> long waves that roughly parallel the long waves in wholesale prices.[22]

The difficulty envisaged by these authors arises from the implicit
assumption that these series would all reflect the long wave in the
same general way. As we have seen earlier, this assumption is not
permissible in the Schumpeterian version of the Kondratieff. It is
worthy of note, furthermore, that only limited observations could
be made for these series. But one upswing is covered, from 1897 to
1919, while the years of downswing were 1879-97 and 1921-33, with
1927-33 omitted in the summary interpretation of findings.[23]

The Problem of Causation

An attempt at comprehensive treatment of the issues associated
with possible explanations of the long waves would take much more
space than we can devote to the matter here. We may, however,
notice two possibilities briefly.

The view that wars are the leading causal factors in producing
the long waves is associated with the name of Ciriacy Wantrup,[24]

---

[21] P. 432.
[22] Pp. 432-433.
[23] P. 435.
[24] See reference in A. Hansen, *Fiscal Policy and Business Cycles*, p. 30n.

though it has also been supported by others.[25]   According to this view, the prosperities preceding wars are to be accounted for in terms of increasing armament expenditures, while the succeeding depressions are attributable to the dislocations ensuing on the curtailment of war expenditures.   This is by no means an adequate account of the theory, and we present it only by way of introduction to a statement of Professor Hansen's.[26]   His analysis led to the following conclusion:

> On balance, it may perhaps be said that, in the "upswing" phase of the first so-called long wave, wars occupied a position of major importance, perhaps equal to that of the innovations introduced by the Industrial Revolution.   Each reinforced the other, and it is difficult to disentangle the relative potency of each factor.   For the second "Aufschwungsspanne" it appears reasonable to conclude that the major factor was the railroadization of the world, and that wars played a relatively minor part, with respect to both the good times and the ensuing period of chronic hard times which followed.   For the third period the most reasonable conclusion appears to be that the electrification and motorization of the Western world played by far the dominant role, reinforced toward the end of the period by the first World War, and that for the succeeding period of economic difficulties postwar readjustments played an important role, though it may well be that the adaptation of the economic structure to the innovational developments of the preceding period was of equal significance.[27]

We shall simply record our agreement with this without going further into the matter.   It may be observed, however, that added stress on the great increases in output in Kondratieff downgrades would still more damage the war explanation.

The general argument that long waves are caused by variations in gold production seems to have lost favor in recent years and, so far as we know, has not been directed against *Business Cycles*.   However, Professor Fels has recently stressed monetary problems in the

---

[25] A. Rose, "Wars, Innovations, and Long Cycles: A Brief Comment," *American Economic Review*, March, 1941, pp. 105-7.   ". . . modern war may be the innovation par excellence in the Schumpeterian system, and as such, the dominant cause of long waves in economic activity."   P. 105. See also N. Silberling, *The Dynamics of Business*, Chapter 4.

[26] Compare also E. Bernstein, "War and the Pattern of Business Cycles," *American Economic Review*, September, 1940, pp. 524-535, especially 534-5.

[27] *Fiscal Policy and Business Cycles*, p. 35.

explanation of "the long-wave depression" of the last quarter of the nineteenth century.[28] We quote:

> . . . in a larger sense we can fit the facts into an old formula—shortage of gold. Had there been more gold production, giving prices an upward impetus, resumption could have been accomplished with less deflation, there would have been meager political support for silver inflation, and bank crises would have been less frequent.[29]

This argument calls for the following comments. (1) Particular events of those years are explained by Professor Schumpeter partly in terms of monetary disturbances, although he does argue that, ". . . barring the effects of the silver experiment, the gold position of the country was favorable, in some years that might have been critical, exceptionally so." [30] (2) In a discussion of debt repayment cited by Professor Fels, Professor Harris observes that from 1866 to 1893 the money supply rose by "about 100 percent." [31] Currency rose from $940 millions to $1,597, while bank deposits rose from $572 millions to $1,574.[32] This reflects a gold shortage in a sense that escapes us, while seeming to bear out the argument of (1) above. (3) Insufficient attention is paid, in this monetary explanation, to the great increases in output in this period, which must have been the main factor influencing the behavior of the price level.

HISTORICAL EPOCHS, BUT NOT CYCLES?

The view that the long waves are historical epochs, not entitled to be called cycles, was early directed against Kondratieff's results by Mitchell and has since been advanced by Mr. Garvy. We may quote Mitchell's criticism:

> Until some adequate reason has been shown why we should expect more or less regular recurrences of "long waves" in economic activities, we shall have nothing beyond empirical evidence concerning their exist-

---

[28] R. Fels, "The Long-Wave Depression, 1873-97," *Review of Economics and Statistics,* February, 1949, pp. 69-73.
[29] P. 70.
[30] *Business Cycles,* p. 318.
[31] S. Harris, *The National Debt and the New Economics,* p. 263.
[32] P. 264.

ence. We may admit the probable validity of Kondratieff's statistical argument that two-and-a-half "long waves" have occurred in various economic processes since the end of the 18th century, and yet hold open the question whether the series will be continued. Two-and-a-half recurrences do not suffice to establish empirically a presumption that any feature of modern history will repeat itself.[33]

Professor Hansen partially agrees with this view, although he has raised some points that serve as objections to it. He says:

Some writers have referred to these prolonged periods of good and bad times as "long waves." Whether or not it is appropriate to do so cannot yet be established in view of the fact that the record reveals thus far only three such "waves," the last of which is yet incomplete and, indeed, in some respects somewhat obscure. It is a fact, however, that as high a degree of periodicity has prevailed for these three waves as any which we find for the major business cycle. Moreover, it is a tenable hypothesis that the process of economic development tends to run not only in terms of the regular business cycle movement, but also in terms of these long waves. Indeed, as also with the business cycle, each phase of these long waves tends, in some measure, though we think less clearly than with respect to the business cycle, automatically to develop into the next succeeding phase.[34]

Professor Schumpeter has taken explicit notice of the argument advanced by Mitchell in the following passage:

Professor Mitchell recognizes the "existence" (on the meaning of this, some remarks will presently be made) of such long movements, but calls them "merely empirical." If the present writer understands correctly, this qualification should be removed by what follows in our text, since reasons will be presented for believing that those movements are associated (to say the least) with definite historical processes in industry which are of the same nature and produce the same symptoms as those which are responsible for and produce the symptoms of cycles which are universally recognized as such.[35]

This note of Professor Schumpeter's is followed by his discussion of the reasons for expecting multiplicity of cycles, in which it is shown that the same process of capitalist development provides a

---

[33] *Business Cycles,* p. 229. See p. 87 above for the remarks of Mr. Garvy.
[34] *Fiscal Policy and Business Cycles,* pp. 29-30.
[35] *Business Cycles,* p. 164n.

rationale for long waves as well as for shorter fluctuations. Thus, on the basis of the criticisms hitherto advanced, there appears to be no valid objection to speaking of long cycles as having occurred in the past. To do so does not, of course, imply anything with regard to the future.

Chapter 11

AN APPRAISAL OF THE SCHUMPETERIAN SYSTEM

Having examined the numerous criticisms that have been made of the Schumpeterian System, we are now in a position to attempt an evaluation of the model as a rendition of capitalist reality. We may conveniently begin with a bald and unqualified summary of the principal conclusions reached in Part Three.

Summary of Conclusions

1. The circular flow of the Pure Model is a valid picture of economic activity in a society corresponding to orthodox conceptions of capitalism with economic change removed.

2. The concept of innovation is logically sound, and is capable of explaining the causation of discontinuous, internal economic change.

3. The theory of the clustering of innovations rests on a firm foundation.

4. A model of capitalist business cycles cannot usefully be based on a theory of employment, or ignore the phenomena associated with the introduction of new production functions.

5. The concepts of both monopoly and competition take on new meaning in the light of the process of creative destruction.

6. The qualitative and quantitative effects of innovation depend alike on the phases of cycles in which they are introduced.

7. Capitalist business cycles are both qualitative and quantitative in nature. The theory of cycles is not analytically separable from the theory of economic development.

8. The three-cycle schema is a useful working model in the analysis of business cycles.

9. The Schumpeterian version of the long wave, with innovation as its primary cause, is a valid approximation to historical reality.

Our more general conclusion must be that all the objections to the Schumpeterian System so far raised fail to damage the model to any discernible extent, and that criticism has left it quite intact.

THEORY AND FACT

Objections to the Schumpeterian System have been raised from the standpoints of both theory and fact. There is, of course, no hard and fast dividing line between these approaches, for theories that are meant to explain facts must emerge from visions of reality.[1]

At the cornerstone of the Schumpeterian System lies the rock of qualitative change on which the theory of economic development is built. This rock provides, moreover, the basis for inevitable disagreement. Qualitative phenomena cannot be excluded from a comprehensive model of the capitalist process, but as soon as they are given considerable emphasis, fallible human judgment must also be admitted in the role of interpreter. It is understandably disappointing, if not frustrating, to those who seek to measure all economic phenomena to come upon this important truth. Where human judgment is involved, differences of opinion cannot be eliminated. That the Schumpeterian System is undamaged by criticism is imperfect proof of its perfection. Further objections may yet be forthcoming. Apart from this, however, the correspondence of the theory to essential fact must be, finally, a matter of opinion.

The empirical foundations of the Schumpeterian System are not all that could be desired. As Professor Schumpeter himself writes, "The younger generation of economists should look upon this book merely as something to shoot at and to start from—as a motivated program for further research." [2] Later on he repeatedly underscores the need for more and better data, studies of firms and industries, historical investigations of entrepreneurship, and innumerable researches of all sorts. The Schumpeterian System is not the ultimate achievement of economic science, and claims of quite another sort are made for it.

The role of empiricism must be seen in its proper light. With

---

[1] It is also true, of course, that even the collection of facts presupposes the existence of some sort of theory. Reference is made to a critical essay of Professor Shaw's for a penetrating discussion of these matters. See E. S. Shaw, "Burns and Mitchell on Business Cycles," *Journal of Political Economy,* August, 1947.

[2] *Business Cycles,* Preface, p. v.

respect to all branches of economic theory, we need incalculable amounts of empirical work. Most of us, however, find it hard to resist a tendency toward naivete in forming our expectations concerning the results of such efforts. With respect to any given model, we shall never prove anything, but only, at most, disprove something.[3] Even then, it is unlikely that our results will be quite conclusive. We need only remind ourselves of the generally inconclusive findings of empirical investigations of such matters as the propensity to consume, demand and supply curves, oligopoly prices, effects of minimum wages, and the validity of marginal analysis. The empirical difficulties associated with the Schumpeterian System are by no means peculiar to that model, but rather permeate the whole fabric of economics.

To say that some parts of the Schumpeterian System are not quantitatively verifiable is not the same as saying that they are not empirically verifiable. We know, for example, that innovations frequently encounter resistance, even though we cannot measure the strength of that resistance with an ohmmeter. Qualitative description here suffices, and is, indeed, all that is possible. To reject a theory on the ground that not all economic data are quantitative is to entertain an incorrect notion of the nature of the subject matter of economics. Moreover, it would amount to abandoning a portion of that subject matter. Such a procedure is legitimate for the specialist, but it nonetheless diminishes the significance of his findings. With respect to those portions of our field that cannot be explored by statistical methods, economists must still hold theories. And these theories may be supported equally well by nonstatistical facts.

Finally, we should do well to remind ourselves occasionally that there is such a thing as the limitations of science. Heaven has not yet been viewed through a telescope, but, after all, what do we expect?

Achievements of the System

We shall not try to catalog the achievements of the Schumpeterian System, but shall content ourselves with noticing four types of contribution that should be particularly remarked. Our comments will be concerned with the following: (1) approximation of the goal;

[3] Compare, G. J. Stigler, *The Theory of Price,* pp. 7-8.

(2) integration of materials; (3) reshaping of the theory of the firm; and (4) illumination of the subject matter of a new discipline. What we have to say about the first of these is simply our own opinion, and we shall state it briefly. For the other three there is adequate support.

1. *Approximation of the goal.* The goal of the Schumpeterian System is the explanation of the process of capitalist economic development. Few models have been constructed with so broad an end in view, and the Schumpeterian System comes closer than any other to achieving it. This model may therefore be taken to mark the region of furthest advance on one of our major lines of effort, and every advantage should be taken of it in attempts at continued progress. If other existing systems are superior, their superiority ought to be shown. As new systems are developed, these too should be tested. Nothing of scientific value is to be gained by neglect of the Schumpeterian System.

2. *Integration of materials.* In undertaking an explanation of the phenomena involved in the capitalist process, Professor Schumpeter has achieved a remarkable integration of materials. Such synthesis occurs on three separate levels. First, there is the integration of three different methods: the theoretical, the historical, and the statistical. This plan of attack is by no means novel in economics, but its advantages have never been better illustrated than in the work of Professor Schumpeter.

Second, the Schumpeterian System affords a means of integrating the many artificial areas of subject matter in our science. The theories of the firm, consumer behavior, credit, profits, interest, equilibrium, business cycles, and economic development—the list is not exhaustive—are interwoven into a logical and connected whole. The simplicity and ease with which these elements fit into a single comprehensive structure definitely count in favor of the system.

Third, substantial progress is made toward the integration of some of the separate disciplines of the social sciences. Attempts in this direction all too often come to nothing for the reason that scholars in one field cannot establish the findings of those in another. Since each field consists of specialized machinery for the discovery of truths, rather than a body of concrete facts, pleas for co-operation among the social sciences have so far borne little fruit. With the realization that co-operation consists, not in the exchange of findings, but in attacks on common problems, the outlook becomes more hopeful. The Schumpeterian System exemplifies the results of this methodology.

3. *Reshaping of the theory of the firm.* Emphasis on innovation and its attendant problems leads to a new approach to the behavior of the firm. Not only are new attitudes evoked toward the traditional problems of the firm, but whole new areas are opened to investigation.

The traditional theory of the firm has to do primarily with the behavior of going concerns, operating within given production functions. The problems of creating the enterprise, and of introducing new methods and new products are commonly ignored or treated in a misleading fashion.[4] We have no intention of questioning the value of exercises in the exploration of the properties of conventional models, but we do contend that preoccupation with these models is frequently excessive, and that their usefulness is diminished by any failure to perceive their limitations.

4. *Illumination of the subject matter of a new discipline.* The Schumpeterian System makes important contributions to the study of economic sociology. If we follow Professor Lange in defining this discipline as "the science of the effect of economic actions upon social actions and relations,"[5] we must recognize that the relation of the entrepreneur to his environment is one of the fundamental problems of the sociology of capitalism. Economic sociology is still in its infancy, but the field is of increasing promise, and Professor Schumpeter's work[6] has done much to reveal its significance. No one who wishes to understand what is happening to capitalism in the modern world need apologize for taking an interest in this study.[7]

---

[4] Some of the consequences of this are visible in the recent debates on marginalism. For an earlier example, contrast the famous discussions about empty economic boxes and increasing returns on the one hand, with "The Instability of Capitalism" on the other.

[5] O. Lange, "The Scope and Method of Economics," *Review of Economic Studies*, 1945-46, p. 19.

[6] Professor Löwe called attention to this fact as early as 1935. See A. Löwe, *Economics and Sociology*, pp. 83ff.

[7] Compare K. E. Boulding, "Samuelson's *Foundations:* The Role of Mathematics in Economics," *Journal of Political Economy*, June, 1948, p. 199.

LIMITATIONS OF THE SYSTEM

We take it to be self-evident that the Schumpeterian System has limitations of the sort inherent in all work in the social sciences. This acknowledgment is not altogether superfluous, for in appraising the merits of a particular model it is easy to employ false criteria. Whether economists know what they are about, and whether their efforts amount to anything, are questions that may be debatable, but not for purposes of this discussion.

Within the area remaining open to consideration, the principal limitation to be recognized is the one deliberately imposed. The Schumpeterian System is a model of the process of a historical epoch that is passing. Large-scale enterprise, large-scale unionism, and large-scale government are hence excluded from the schema. The analysis seems, therefore, to be more immediately useful to the economic historian than to students of the contemporary scene. To be sure, present developments acquire meaning only in the light of the past, but beyond this there remains the question of the persistence of capitalist patterns of behavior.[8]

Trustified Capitalism and the Laboristic Society[9] are two sides of the same coin, and the coin itself bears various names, of which one is collectivism. Our hopes and fears, however, are likely to dim our vision. The capitalism of the Schumpeterian System is not yet dead in America, and the model will continue to have relevance for some time to come. The precise extent of this relevance must be a matter

---

[8] For a discussion of some aspects of this question see D. M. Wright, "The Prospects for Capitalism," *A Survey of Contemporary Economics,* Chapter 13. For Professor Schumpeter's views see *Capitalism, Socialism, and Democracy,* Part II. We cannot go into the matter here beyond pointing out that the Schumpeterian thesis has not been successfully challenged. O. H. Taylor, "The Economics of a 'Free' Society," *Quarterly Journal of Economics,* November, 1948, p. 649, refers to Chapter II of Professor Jewkes's *Ordeal by Planning* as "a fairly cogent refutation" of the thesis. Professor Schumpeter, however, failed to recognize his own argument in the statements attacked. See J. A. Schumpeter, "English Economists and the State-Managed Economy," *Journal of Political Economy,* October, 1949, p. 374, n. 6.

[9] See S. H. Slichter, *The American Economy,* pp. 7-13 and 211-214.

of opinion, so that some will think it necessary to start afresh, while others will prefer to undertake alterations.

From the standpoint of its applicability to public policy the limitations of the Schumpeterian System are apparent. Here we are concerned with the question of alternatives, however, and it is not clear that concessions would be appropriate. The truth is that no economic models are reliable guides to policy, and the more that is claimed for them the more they are suspect. We get out of any model only what we put into it, and to the extent that assumptions are identified and their implications appreciated, illusions to the contrary are dispelled. To pursue this line of thought any further would take us outside the area to which this discussion is confined. Councils of advisors and policymakers have their work to do, and their problems are not, in any event, wholly economic. On the broader questions of policy the Schumpeterian System sheds a good deal of light,[10] and it also provides a comprehensive frame of reference into which other models may be fitted.[11]

On the whole it appears that the deliberate limitation of Professor Schumpeter's model to the historical past amounts to a recognition of the fact that synthesis can be attempted only after the returns are in. Since this is the only way we have of illuminating the present, it can hardly be called an objection to the Schumpeterian System.

---

[10] The scientific detachment with which the model is presented has been the source of some difficulty. Professor Kierstead, for example, finds the Schumpeterian outlook unduly optimistic (*Theory of Economic Change,* p. 97), whereas Professor Wright (*A Survey of Contemporary Economics,* p. 471) thinks it too pessimistic. Needless to say, the optimism or pessimism is in the mind of the reader, and not in the analysis itself. Both friends and foes of capitalism who are in search of effective programs can hardly fail to profit by an examination of *Business Cycles* and *Capitalism, Socialism, and Democracy.*

[11] No one need sacrifice the real advantages of aggregative analysis, for instance, in order to accept the Schumpeterian System.

BIBLIOGRAPHY

ACHINSTEIN, A., *Introduction to Business Cycles,* New York, Crowell, 1950.

ADAMS, M., "The Automobile—a Luxury Becomes a Necessity," Hamilton and Associates, *Price and Price Policies,* New York and London, McGraw-Hill, 1938, Sec. II, pp. 27-81.

AFTALION, A., "The Theory of Economic Cycles Based on the Capitalistic Technique of Production," *Review of Economic Statistics,* October, 1927, pp. 165-170.

AMERICAN ECONOMIC ASSOCIATION, *Readings in Business Cycle Theory,* Philadelphia and Toronto, Blakiston, 1944.

AMERICAN ECONOMIC ASSOCIATION, *Readings in the Theory of Income Distribution,* Philadelphia and Toronto, Blakiston, 1946.

AMES, E., "A Theoretical and Statistical Dilemma—The Contributions of Burns, Mitchell, and Frickey to Business-Cycle Theory," *Econometrica,* July, 1948, pp. 347-369.

ANGELL, J. W., "Current Research in Business Cycles—Discussion," *American Economic Review,* Supplement, May, 1949, pp. 73-77.

ANGELL, J. W., *Investment and Business Cycles,* New York and London, McGraw-Hill, 1941.

ASHTON, T. S., *The Industrial Revolution,* New York and London, Oxford University Press, 1948.

ASHTON, T. S., "The Relation of Economic History to Economic Theory," *Economica,* May, 1946, pp. 81-96.

AYRES, C. E., *The Theory of Economic Progress,* Chapel Hill, University of North Carolina Press, 1944.

BAIN, J. S., "Market Classifications in Modern Price Theory," *Quarterly Journal of Economics,* August, 1942, pp. 562-565.

BEALES, H. L., "The 'Great Depression' in Industry and Trade," *Economic History Review,* October, 1934, pp. 65-75.

BENNION, E. G., "Unemployment in the Theories of Schumpeter and Keynes," *American Economic Review,* June, 1943, pp. 336-347.

BERNSTEIN, E. M., "War and the Pattern of Business Cycles," *American Economic Review,* September, 1940, pp. 324-335.

BLAIR, J. M., "Technology and Size," *American Economic Review,* Supplement, May, 1948, pp. 121-152.

BOULDING, K. E., "In Defense of Monopoly," *Quarterly Journal of Economics,* August, 1945, pp. 524-542.

BOULDING, K. E., "Samuelson's *Foundations:* The Role of Mathematics in Economics," *Journal of Political Economy,* June, 1948, pp. 187-199.

BRATT, E. C., *Business Cycles and Forecasting,* Chicago, Irwin, 3d ed., 1948.

BRONFENBRENNER, M., "The Introductory Course: Comment," *American Economic Review,* September, 1942, pp. 557-558.

BUCHANAN, N. S., "Anticipations and Industrial Investment Decisions," *American Economic Review*, Supplement, March, 1942, pp. 141-155.

BUCHANAN, N. S., "Theory of Fluctuation in Business Profits," *American Economic Review*, December, 1941, pp. 731-753.

BURNS, A. F., "Current Research in Business Cycles—Discussion," *American Economic Review*, Supplement, May 1949, pp. 77-83.

BURNS, A. F., *Production Trends in the United States Since 1870*, New York, National Bureau of Economic Research, 1934.

BURNS, A. F., and MITCHELL, W. C., *Measuring Business Cycles*, New York, National Bureau of Economic Research, 1946.

CLAPHAM, J. H., "Of Empty Economic Boxes," *Economic Journal*, September, 1922, pp. 305-314.

CLARK, C., *The Economics of 1960*, London, Macmillan, 1942.

CLARK, J. B., Review of Schumpeter's *Theorie der Wirtschaftlichen Entwicklung*, American Economic Review, December, 1912, pp. 873-875.

CLARK, J. M., "Relations of History and Theory," *Journal of Economic History*, Supplement II, 1942, pp. 132-142.

CLEMENCE, R. V., and DOODY, F. S., "Modern Economics and the Introductory Course," *American Economic Review*, June, 1942, pp. 334-347.

COLE, A. H., "An Approach to the Study of Entrepreneurship: A Tribute to Edwin F. Gay," *Journal of Economic History*, Supplement VI, 1946, pp. 1-15.

COLE, A. H., "Entrepreneurship as an Area of Research," *Journal of Economic History*, Supplement II, 1942, pp. 118-126.

COMMITTEE ON PRICE DETERMINATION FOR THE CONFERENCE ON PRICE RESEARCH, *Cost Behavior and Price Policy*, New York, National Bureau of Economic Research, 1943.

DAVIS, H. S., *The Industrial Study of Economic Progress*, Philadelphia, University of Pennsylvania Press, 1947.

DESTLER, C. M., "Entrepreneurial Leadership Among the 'Robber Barons': A Trial Balance," *Journal of Economic History*, Supplement VI, 1946, pp. 28-49.

DEWEY, E. R., and DAKIN, E. F., *Cycles: The Science of Prediction*, New York, Holt, 1947.

DUE, J. F., *Intermediate Economic Analysis*, Chicago, Irwin, 1947.

DUNLOP, J. T., "The Development of Labor Organization: A Theoretical Framework," *Insights into Labor Issues*, Ed. Lester and Shister, New York, Macmillan, 1948, pp. 163-193.

EAST, R. A., "The Business Entrepreneur in a Changing Colonial Economy, 1763-1795," *Journal of Economic History*, Supplement VI, 1946, pp. 16-27.

EASTERBROOK, W. T., "The Climate of Enterprise," *American Economic Review*, Supplement, May, 1949, pp. 322-335.

ELLIS, H. S. (ed.), *A Survey of Contemporary Economics*, Philadelphia and Toronto, Blakiston, 1948.

ELLIS, H. S., *German Monetary Theory*, 1905-1933, Cambridge, Harvard University Press, 1934.

ELLIS, H. S., "Monopoly and Unemployment," *Prices, Wages, and Employment*, Postwar Economic Studies No. 4, Washington, Board of Governors of the Federal Reserve System, May, 1946, pp. 67-94.

ELLIS, H. S., "The State of the 'New Economics,' " *American Economic Review*, March, 1949, pp. 465-477.

EPSTEIN, R. C., "Industrial Invention: Heroic or Systematic?" *Quarterly Journal of Economics*, February, 1926, pp. 232-272.

ESTEY, J. A., *Business Cycles: Their Nature, Cause, and Control*, New York, Prentice-Hall, 2d ed., 1950.

EVANS, G. H., JR., "A Theory of Entrepreneurship," *Journal of Economic History*, Supplement II, 1942, pp. 142-146.

EVANS, G. H., JR., "The Entrepreneur and Economic Theory: A Historical and Analytical Approach," *American Economic Review*, Supplement, May, 1949, pp. 336-348.

FELLNER, W. J., *Monetary Policies and Full Employment*, Berkeley and Los Angeles, University of California Press, 1946.

FELS, R., "The Long-Wave Depression, 1873-97," *Review of Economics and Statistics*, February, 1949, pp. 69-73.

FISHER, A. G. B., *Economic Progress and Social Security*, London, Macmillan, 1945.

FISHER, A. G. B., *The Clash of Progress and Security*, London, Macmillan, 1935.

FRICKEY, E., *Economic Fluctuations in the United States: A Systematic Analysis of Long-Run Trends and Business Cycles, 1866-1914*, Cambridge, Harvard University Press, 1942.

FRISCH, R., "On the Notion of Equilibrium and Disequilibrium," *Review of Economic Studies*, III, 1935-1936, pp. 100-106.

FRISCH, R., "Propagation Problems and Impluse Problems in Dynamic Economics," *Economic Essays in Honour of Gustav Cassel*, London, Allen and Unwin, 1933.

GARVY, G., "Kondratieff's Theory of Long Cycles," *Review of Economic Statistics*, November, 1943, pp. 203-220.

GIDE, C., and RIST, C., *A History of Economic Doctrines from the Time of the Physiocrats to the Present Day*, Boston, Heath, 2d English ed., 1948.

GILFILLAN, S. C., "Invention as a Factor in Economic History," *Journal of Economic History*, Supplement V, 1945, pp. 66-85.

GILFILLAN, S. C., "The Prediction of Inventions," *Technological Trends and National Policy*, Washington, National Resources Committee, 1937, pp. 15-23.

GILFILLAN, S. C., *The Sociology of Invention*, Chicago, Follett, 1935.

GLENDAY, R., "Long Period Economic Trends," *Journal of The Royal Statistical Society*, Part III, 1938, pp. 511-552.

GLENDAY, R., *The Future of Economic Society: A Study in Group Organization*, London, Macmillan, 1944.

GOODWIN, R., "Innovations and the Irregularity of Economic Cycles," *Review of Economic Statistics*, May, 1946, pp. 95-104.

GORDON, R. A., "Business Cycles in the Interwar Period: The 'Quantitative-Historical' Approach," *American Economic Review*, Supplement, May, 1949, pp. 47-63.

GOURVITCH, A., *Survey of Economic Theory on Technological Change and Emplyoment*, Philadelphia, WPA National Resources Project, 1940.

GRAS, N. S. B., *Business and Capitalism: An Introduction to Business History*, New York, Crofts, 1939.

GRAS, N. S. B., and LARSON, H. M., *Casebook in American Business History*, New York, Crofts, 1939.

HAAVELMO, T., "Statistical Testing of Business-Cycle Theories," *Review of Economic Statistics*, February, 1943, pp. 13-18.

HABERLER, G., "Current Research in Business Cycles—Discussion," *American Economic Review*, Supplement, May, 1949, pp. 84-88.

HABERLER, G., *Prosperity and Depression: A Theoretical Analysis of Cyclical Movements*, Lake Success, United Nations, 3d ed., 1946.

HABERLER, G., "The Interest Rate and Capital Formation," *Capital Formation and Its Elements*, National Industrial Conference Board, 1939, pp. 119-133.

HANCE, W. E., "The Role of the Automobile Industry," *American Economic Review*, Supplement, March, 1939, pp. 42-44.

HANEY, L. H., *History of Economic Thought: A Critical Account of the Origin and Development of the Economic Theories of the Leading Thinkers in the Leading Nations*, New York, Macmillan, 4th ed., 1949.

HANSEN, A. H., *Business-Cycle Theory*, Boston, Ginn, 1927.

HANSEN, A. H., *Economic Stabilization in an Unbalanced World*, New York, Harcourt, Brace, 1932.

HANSEN, A. H., *Fiscal Policy and Business Cycles*, New York, Norton, 1941.

HANSEN, A. H., Review of Schumpeter's *Theory of Economic Development*, *Journal of Political Economy*, August, 1936, pp. 560-563.

HANSEN, A. H., "Some Notes on Terborgh's 'The Bogey of Economic Maturity,'" *Review of Economic Statistics*, February, 1946, pp. 13-17.

HANSEN, A. H., "The Business Depression of Nineteen-Hundred Thirty," Discussion, *American Economic Review*, Supplement, March, 1931, pp. 198-201.

HARDY, C. O., *Is There Enough Gold?* Washington, Brookings Institution, 1936.

HARDY, C. O., "Schumpeter on Capitalism, Socialism, and Democracy," *Journal of Political Economy*, December, 1945, pp. 348-356.

HARRIS, S. E., *The National Debt and the New Economics*, New York and London, McGraw-Hill, 1947.

HAYEK, F. A., "Investment That Raises the Demand for Capital," *Review of Economic Statistics*, November, 1937, pp. 174-177.

HEIMANN, E., *History of Economic Doctrines*, New York, Oxford University Press, 1945.

HENDERSON, W. O., "Trade Cycles in the 19th Century," *History*, July, 1933, pp. 147-153.

HICKS, J. R., *Value and Capital: An Inquiry into Some Fundamental Principles of Economic Theory*, Oxford, Clarendon Press, 2d ed., 1946.

HIGGINS, B., "Concepts and Criteria of Secular Stagnation," *Income, Employment, and Public Policy*, New York, Norton, 1948, pp. 82-107.

HILDEBRAND, G. H., Jr., "Monopolization and the Decline of Investment Opportunity," *American Economic Review*, September, 1943, pp. 591-601.

HOUGHTON, H. F., "The Growth of Big Business," *American Economic Review*, Supplement, May, 1948, pp. 72-93.

HUTCHISON, T. W., "A Note on Tautologies and the Nature of Economic Theory," *Review of Economic Studies*, Vol. II, 1934-1935, pp. 159-161.

HUTCHISON, T. W., *The Significance and Basic Postulates of Economic Theory*, London, Macmillan, 1938.

HYSON, C. D., and SANDERSON, F. H., "Monopolistic Discrimination in the Cranberry Industry," *Quarterly Journal of Economics*, May, 1945, pp. 330-369.

INNIS, H. A., Review of Schumpeter's *Business Cycles, Canadian Journal of Economics and Political Science*, February, 1940, pp. 90-96.

ISARD, W., "A Neglected Cycle: The Transport-Building Cycle," *Review of Economic Statistics*, November, 1942, pp. 149-158.

ISARD, W., "Transport Development and Building Cycles," *Quarterly Journal of Economics*, November, 1942, pp. 90-112.

ISARD, W., and ISARD, C., "The Transport-Building Cycle in Urban Development: Chicago," *Review of Economic Statistics*, November, 1943, pp. 224-226.

ISE, J., "The Futility of Trust-Busting," *American Economic Review*, Supplement, May, 1948, pp. 488-501.

JENKS, L. H., "Railroads as an Economic Force in American Development," *Journal of Economic History*, May, 1944, pp. 1-20.

JEWKES, J., *Ordeal by Planning*, London, Macmillan, 1948.

JONES, M. V., *Secular Trends and Idle Resources*, Chicago, University of Chicago Press, 1944.

KENDALL, M. G., Review of Schumpeter's *Business Cycles, Journal of the Royal Statistical Society*, Vol. CIV, Part II, 1941, pp. 177-180.

KEYNES, J. M., "Alfred Marshall, 1842-1924," *Memorials of Alfred Marshall*, Ed. Pigou, pp. 1-65.

KEYNES, J. M., *A Treatise on Money*, New York, Harcourt, Brace, 1930.

KEYNES, J. M., *The General Theory of Employment, Interest, and Money*, New York, Harcourt, Brace, 1936.

KIERSTEAD, B. S., *The Theory of Economic Change*, Toronto, Macmillan, 1949.

KITCHIN, J., "Cycles and Trends in Economic Factors," *Review of Economic Statistics*, January, 1923, pp. 10-16.

KLEIN, L., *The Keynesian Revolution*, New York, Macmillan, 1947.

KNIGHT, F. H., "Diminishing Returns from Investment," *Journal of Political Economy*, March, 1944, pp. 26-47.

KNIGHT, F. H., "Profit and Entrepreneurial Functions," *Journal of Economic History*, Supplement II, 1942, pp. 126-132.

KONDRATIEFF, N. D., "The Long Waves in Economic Life," *Review of Economic Statistics*, November, 1935, pp. 105-115.

KONDRATIEFF, N. D., "The Static and the Dynamic View of Economics," *Quarterly Journal of Economics*, August, 1925, pp. 575-583.

KUZNETS, S. S., "Equilibrium Economics and Business Cycle Theory," *Quarterly Journal of Economics*, May, 1930, pp. 381-419.

KUZNETS, S. S., *National Income: A Summary of Findings*, New York, National Bureau of Economic Research, 1946.

KUZNETS, S. S., *National Product Since 1869*, New York, National Bureau of Economic Research, 1946.

KUZNETS, S. S., Review of Hansen's *Fiscal Policy and Business Cycles*, *Review of Economic Statistics*, February, 1942, pp. 31-36.

KUZNETS, S. S., "Schumpeter's Business Cycles," *American Economic Review*, June, 1940, pp. 257-271.

KUZNETS, S. S., *Secular Movements in Production and Prices: Their Nature and Their Bearing Upon Cyclical Fluctuations*, Boston, Houghton Mifflin, 1930.

KUZNETS, S. S., "Statistics and Economic History," *Journal of Economic History*, May, 1941, pp. 26-41.

LACHMANN, L. M., "Investment Repercussions," *Quarterly Journal of Economics*, November, 1948, pp. 698-713.

LANGE, O., "A Note on Innovations," *Review of Economic Statistics*, February, 1943, pp. 19-25.

LANGE, O., Review of Schumpeter's *Business Cycles*, *Review of Economic Statistics*, November, 1941, pp. 190-193.

LANGE, O., "The Scope and Method of Economics," *Review of Economic Studies*, 1945-1946, pp. 19-32.

LEONTIEF, W., "Implicit Theorizing: A Methodological Criticism of the Neo-Cambridge School," *Quarterly Journal of Economics*, February, 1937, pp. 337-351.

LÖSCH, A., "Population Cycles as a Cause of Business Cycles," *Quarterly Journal of Economics*, August, 1937, pp. 649-662.

LÖWE, A., *Economics and Sociology: A Plea for Co-operation in the Social Sciences*, London, Allen and Unwin, 1935.

MACAULAY, F. R., *Some Theoretical Problems Suggested by the Movements of Interest Rates, Bond Yields and Stock Prices in the United States Since 1856*, New York, National Bureau of Economic Research, 1938.

MACHINERY AND ALLIED PRODUCTS INSTITUTE, *An Appraisal of the Fatalistic View of Capitalism*, Chicago, 1944.

MACHLUP, F., "Capitalism and Its Future Appraised by Two Liberal Economists," *American Economic Review*, June, 1943, pp. 301-320.

MARGET, A. W., *The Theory of Prices: A Re-examination of the Central Problems of Monetary Theory*, New York, Prentice-Hall, Vol. I, 1938, Vol. II, 1942.

MARSHAK, J., "A Cross Section of Business Cycle Discussion," *American Economic Review*, June, 1945, pp. 368-381.

MARSHAK, J., Review of Schumpeter's *Business Cycles, Journal of Political Economy,* December, 1940, pp. 889-894.

MARSHALL, A., *Principles of Economics,* London, Macmillan, 8th ed., 1920.

MARTIN, R. F., *National Income in the United States, 1799-1938,* New York, National Industrial Conference Board, 1939.

MASON, E. S., "Price and Production Policies of Large-Scale Enterprise," *American Economic Review,* Supplement, March, 1939, pp. 61-74.

McCRACKEN, H. L., *Value Theory and Business Cycles,* New York and London, McGraw-Hill, 2d ed., 1936.

McCREA, R. C., "Schumpeter's Economic System," *Quarterly Journal of Economics,* May, 1913, pp. 520-529.

MERLIN, S. D., *The Theory of Fluctuations in Contemporary Economic Thought,* New York, Columbia University Press, 1949.

MERTON, R. K., "Fluctuations in the Rate of Industrial Invention," *Quarterly Journal of Economics,* May, 1935, pp. 454-474.

METZLER, L. A., "Business Cycles and the Modern Theory of Employment," *American Economic Review,* June, 1946, pp. 278-291.

METZLER, L. A., "Keynes and the Theory of Business Cycles," *The New Economics,* Ed. Harris, New York, Knopf, 1947, pp. 436-449.

METZLER, L. A., "The Nature and Stability of Inventory Cycles," *Review of Economic Statistics,* August, 1941, pp. 113-129.

MILL, J. S., *Principles of Political Economy with Some of Their Applications to Social Philosophy,* Ed. Ashley, London, Longmans, 1929.

MIRKOWICH, N., "Schumpeter's Theory of Economic Development," *American Economic Review,* September, 1940, p. 580.

MITCHELL, W. C., *Business Cycles: The Problem and Its Setting,* New York, National Bureau of Economic Research, 1927.

MORGENSTERN, O., Review of Schumpeter's *Business Cycles, Journal of the American Statistical Association,* June, 1940, pp. 423-424.

MOULTON, H. G., "Commercial Banking and Capital Formation," *Journal of Political Economy,* June, 1918, pp. 656-668.

MOULTON, H. G., *Controlling Factors in Economic Development,* Washington, Brookings Institution, 1949.

PIGOU, A. C., "An Analysis of Supply," *Economic Journal,* June, 1928.

PIGOU, A. C., "Empty Economic Boxes: A Reply," *Economic Journal,* December, 1922, pp. 458-465.

PIGOU, A. C. (ed.), *Memorials of Alfred Marshall,* London, Macmillan, 1925.

PIGOU, A. C., "The Laws of Diminishing and Increasing Cost," *Economic Journal,* June, 1927, pp. 188-197.

RESEARCH CENTER IN ENTREPRENEURIAL HISTORY, *Change and the Entrepreneur,* Cambridge, Harvard University Press, 1949.

ROBBINS, L., *An Essay on the Nature and Significance of Economic Science,* London, Macmillan, 2d ed., 1935.

ROBBINS, L., "On a Certain Ambiguity in the Conception of Stationary Equilibrium," *Economic Journal,* June, 1930, pp. 194-214.

ROBBINS, L., "The Representative Firm," *Economic Journal,* September, 1928.

ROBERTSON, D. H., "Those Empty Boxes," *Economic Journal*, March, 1924, pp. 16-31.

ROBERTSON, D. H., SHOVE, G. F., and SRAFFA, P., "Increasing Returns and the Representative Firm: A Symposium," *Economic Journal*, March, 1930, pp. 79-116.

ROLL, E., *A History of Economic Thought*, New York, Prentice-Hall, 1942.

ROSE, A., "Wars, Innovations and Long Cycles: A Brief Comment," *American Economic Review*, March, 1941, pp. 105-107.

ROSTOW, W. W., *British Economy of the Nineteenth Century*, New York, Oxford University Press, 1948.

ROTHBARTH, E., Review of Schumpeter's *Business Cycles*, *Economic Journal*, June-September, 1942, pp. 223-229.

SAMUELSON, P. A., *Foundations of Economic Analysis*, Cambridge, Harvard University Press, 1947.

SAMUELSON, P. A., "Dynamics, Statics, and the Stationary State," *Review of Economic Statistics*, February, 1943, pp. 58-68.

SCHUMPETER, J. A., "Alfred Marshall's *Principles*: A Semi-Centennial Appraisal," *American Economic Review*, June, 1941, pp. 236-248.

SCHUMPETER, J. A., "A Theorist's Comment on the Current Business Cycle," *Journal of the American Statistical Association*, Supplement, 1935, pp. 167-168.

SCHUMPETER, J. A., *Business Cycles: A Theoretical, Historical, and Statistical Analysis of the Capitalist Process*, New York and London, McGraw-Hill, 1939.

SCHUMPETER, J. A., *Capitalism, Socialism, and Democracy*, New York, Harper & Bros., Rev. ed., 1947.

SCHUMPETER, J. A., "Capitalism in the Postwar World," *Postwar Economic Problems*, Ed. Harris, New York and London, McGraw-Hill, 1943, Chap. VI, pp. 113-126.

SCHUMPETER, J. A., "Depressions," *The Economics of the Recovery Program*, Ed. Brown, New York and London, Whittlesey House, McGraw-Hill, 1934, pp. 3-21.

SCHUMPETER, J. A., "Economic Theory and Entrepreneurial History," *Change and the Entrepreneur*, Research Center in Entrepreneurial History, Harvard University, Cambridge, Harvard University Press, 1949, pp. 63-84.

SCHUMPETER, J. A., "English Economists and the State-Managed Economy," *Journal of Political Economy*, October, 1949, pp. 371-382.

SCHUMPETER, J. A., "John Maynard Keynes: 1883-1946," *American Economic Review*, September, 1946, pp. 495-518.

SCHUMPETER, J. A., "Mitchell's Business Cycles," *Quarterly Journal of Economics*, November, 1930, pp. 150-172.

SCHUMPETER, J. A., "On the Concept of Social Value," *Quarterly Journal of Economics*, February, 1909, pp. 213-232.

SCHUMPETER, J. A., Review of Hayek's *The Road to Serfdom*, *Journal of Political Economy*, April, 1946, pp. 269-270.

SCHUMPETER, J. A., Review of H. J. Laski, *Reflections on the Revolution of Our Time, American Economic Review,* March, 1944, pp. 161-164.

SCHUMPETER, J. A., Review of Keynes's *General Theory, Journal of the American Statistical Association,* December, 1936, pp. 791-795.

SCHUMPETER, J. A., "Robinson's Economics of Imperfect Competition," *Journal of Political Economy,* April, 1934, pp. 249-257.

SCHUMPETER, J. A., "Science and Ideology," *American Economic Review,* March, 1949, pp. 345-359.

SCHUMPETER, J. A., "The Analysis of Economic Change," *Review of Economic Statistics,* May, 1935, pp. 2-10.

SCHUMPETER, J. A., "The *Communist Manifesto* in Sociology and Economics," *Journal of Political Economy,* June, 1949, pp. 199-212.

SCHUMPETER, J. A., "The Creative Response in Economic History," *Journal of Economic History,* November, 1947, pp. 149-159.

SCHUMPETER, J. A., "The Decade of the Twenties," *American Economic Review,* Supplement, May, 1946, pp. 1-10.

SCHUMPETER, J. A., "The Explanation of the Business Cycle," *Economica,* December, 1927, pp. 286-311.

SCHUMPETER, J. A., "The Instability of Capitalism," *Economic Journal,* September, 1928, pp. 361-386.

SCHUMPETER, J. A., "The Nature and Necessity of a Price System," *Economic Reconstruction,* New York, Columbia University Press, 1934, pp. 170-176.

SCHUMPETER, J. A., "Theoretical Problems of Economic Growth," *Journal of Economic History,* Supplement VII, 1947, pp. 1-9.

SCHUMPETER, J. A., *Theorie der wirtschlaftlichen Entwicklung,* Leipsig, Duncker und Humblot, 2d ed., 1926.

SCHUMPETER, J. A., *The Theory of Economic Development: An Inquiry into Profits, Capital, Credit, Interest, and the Business Cycle,* Cambridge, Harvard University Press, 1936.

SCHUMPETER, J. A., "The Present World Depression: A Tentative Diagnosis," *American Economic Review,* Supplement, March, 1931, pp. 179-183.

SCHUMPETER, J. A., "Unternehmer," *Handwörterbuch der Staatswissenschaften,* Vierte Auflage, VIII, Jena, Gustav Fischer, 1923, pp. 476-487.

SHAW, E. S., "Burns and Mitchell on Business Cycles," *Journal of Political Economy,* August, 1947, pp. 281-298.

SILBERLING, N. J., *The Dynamics of Business: An Analysis of Trends, Cycles, and Time Relationships in American Economic Activity Since 1700 and Their Bearing upon Governmental and Business Policy,* New York and London, McGraw-Hill, 1943.

SLICHTER, S. H., *The American Economy: Its Problems and Prospects,* New York, Knopf, 1948.

SMITH, W. B., and COLE, A. H., *Fluctuations in American Business, 1790-1860,* Cambridge, Harvard University Press, 1935.

SOMBART, W., "Capitalism," *Encyclopedia of the Social Sciences,* III, 203.

SOUTER, R. W., "Equilibrium Economics and Business Cycle Theory: A

Commentary," *Quarterly Journal of Economics*, November, 1930, pp. 40-93.

SRAFFA, P., "The Laws of Returns under Competitive Conditions," *Economic Journal*, December, 1926, pp. 535-550.

STAUSS, J. H., "The Entrepreneur: The Firm," *Journal of Political Economy*, June, 1944, pp. 112-127.

STERN, B. J., "Resistances to the Adoption of Technological Innovations," *Technological Trends and National Policy*, Washington, National Resources Committee, 1937, pp. 39-66.

STIGLER, G. J., *The Theory of Price*, New York, Macmillan, 1946.

STOLPER, W. F., "Monetary, Equilibrium, and Business-Cycle Theory," *Review of Economic Statistics*, February, 1943, pp. 88-92.

STOLPER, W. F., "The Possibility of Equilibrium under Monopolistic Competition," *Quarterly Journal of Economics*, May, 1940, pp. 519-526.

SURANYI-UNGER, T., *Economics in the Twentieth Century: The History of Its International Development*, New York, Norton, 1931.

SWANSON, E. W., and SCHMIDT, E. P., *Economic Stagnation or Progress: A Critique of Recent Doctrines on the Mature Economy, Oversavings, and Deficit Spending*, New York and London, McGraw-Hill, 1946.

SWEEZY, P. M., "Professor Schumpeter's Theory of Innovation," *Review of Economic Statistics*, February, 1943, pp. 93-96.

SWEEZY, P. M., *Socialism*, New York, McGraw-Hill, 1949.

SWEEZY, P. M., *The Theory of Capitalist Development: Principles of Marxian Political Economy*, New York, Oxford University Press, 1942.

TAUSSIG, F. W., "Capital, Interest, and Diminishing Returns," *Quarterly Journal of Economics*, May, 1908, pp. 333-363.

TAYLOR, O. H., "The Economics of a 'Free' Society: Four Essays," *Quarterly Journal of Economics*, November, 1948, pp. 641-670.

TAYMANS, A. C., "George Tarde and Joseph A. Schumpeter: A Similar Vision," *Explorations in Entrepreneurial History*, Research Center in Entrepreneurial History, Harvard University, Vol. I, No. 4, April, 1949, pp. 9-17, mimeographed.

TERBORGH, G., *The Bogey of Economic Maturity*, Chicago, Machinery and Allied Products Institute, 1945.

THORP, W. L., *Business Annals*, New York, National Bureau of Economic Research, 1926.

THORP, W. L., "The Business Depression of Nineteen-Hundred Thirty," Discussion, *American Economic Review*, Supplement, March, 1931, pp. 196-198.

TNEC: *Savings and Investment*, Testimony of A. H. Hansen, pp. 3495-3520, 3538-3559 (deficit financing), 3837-3859 (capital budget).

USHER, A. P., *A History of Mechanical Inventions*, New York and London, McGraw-Hill, 1929.

USHER, A. P., "The Significance of Modern Empiricism for History and Economics," *Journal of Economic History*, November, 1949, pp. 137-155.

VEBLEN, T., *The Theory of Business Enterprise*, New York, Scribner's, 1904.

VON MISES, L., *Human Action*, New Haven, Yale University Press, 1949.

WAGEMANN, E., *Economic Rhythm: A Theory of Business Cycles,* New York and London, McGraw-Hill, 1930.

WARRINER, D., "Schumpeter and the Conception of Static Equilibrium," *Economic Journal,* March, 1931, pp. 38-50.

WELLS, D. A., *Recent Economic Changes and Their Effect on the Production and Distribution of Wealth and the Well-Being of Society,* New York, Appleton, 1890.

WHITTAKER, E., *A History of Economic Ideas,* New York, Longmans, Green, 1940.

WICKSELL, K., *Interest and Prices: A Study of the Causes Regulating the Value of Money,* Trans. Kahn, London, Macmillan, 1936.

WILSON, T., *Fluctuations in Income and Employment,* New York and London, Pitman, 3d ed., 1948.

WRIGHT, C. D., *Industrial Depressions: Annual Report of the Commissioner of Labor,* Washington, 1886.

WRIGHT, D. M., *Democracy and Progress,* New York, Macmillan, 1948.

WRIGHT, D. M., "Mr. Harrod and Growth Economics," *Review of Economics and Statistics,* November, 1949, pp. 322-328.

WRIGHT, D. M., "Professor Knight on Limits to the Use of Capital," *Quarterly Journal of Economics,* May, 1944, pp. 331-358.

WRIGHT, D. M., *The Economics of Disturbance,* New York, Macmillan, 1947.

YOUNG, A. A., "Increasing Returns and Economic Progress," *Economic Journal,* December, 1928, pp. 527-542.

INDEX

Hawtrey, R. G., 70
Hayek, F., 64n
Henderson, W. O., 45n
Hermann, E., 28n
Hildebrand, G. H., Jr., 63n
Historic time, 68, 69
History, 45, 68, 73

Ignition, 67
Imperfect competition, 16, 61-63
Induced investment, 16, 64-68
Inflection points, 77, 78
Innis, H. A., 3n
Innovation and circular flow, 27, 32
Innovation and long waves, 87-91
Innovation clustering, 51f
Innovation definition, 9, 36, 37-41
Innovation, single cause?, 48-50, 89, 90
    too broad?, 41, 42
    too narrow?, 42-46
Innovations
    why innovated?, 46-48
Institutional character of model, 11, 33-35, 47, 99, 100
Interest, 28f
Invention, 38
Investment opportunity, 64-69
Isard, W., 68n, 81, 82

Jewkes, J., 99n
Jones, M. V., 55n
Juglar, C., 20
Juglars, 20, 60, 61, 79

Kendall, M. G., 3n
Keynes, J. M., 25n, 59-61

Kierstead, B. S., 31, 32, 43, 44, 48, 50n, 100n
Kitchin, J., 20, 75
Kitchins, 20, 60, 61, 79
Klein, L., 61n
Kondratieff, N., 20, 75n, 76, 77, 83, 87
Kondratieffs, 44n, 79, 81, 82, 83f
Kuznets, S., 3n, 39n, 52, 53, 69, 74n, 77n, 78n, 85-87

Lachmann, L. M., 64
Lange, O., 5n, 41, 42, 55, 59, 79, 98
Larson, H. M., 88n
Lerner, A. P., 3n
Leontief, W., 39n
Limit of capital, 29, 30
Lowe, A., 98n

Maintenance of capital, 28, 29
Marget, A., 3, 4n
Marshak, J., 3n, 5n
Marshall, A., 25n, 45n
Marxist point of view, 33-35, 46, 61, 62
Mason, E. S., 63n
Merlin, S. D., 38n
Metzler, L., 61n, 79n
Mill, J. S., 25, 26
Mirkowich, N., 4n
Mitchell, W. C., 61n, 83, 89, 91, 92
Monopoly, 61-63
Morgenstern, D., 3n
Moulton, H. G., 4n
Multiple cycles, 18-21, 75f, 88

National income analysis, 4, 5, 87
New firms, 9, 40, 53, 54